This book by Dr. Daniel Morris is a tremendous writing, dealing with temptation and how to overcome it. The research is very thorough and includes a practical description of temptation and its effect on the believer. I recommend this book not only for those overcome with temptations, but also as a tool in helping someone else who is dealing with these issues. He clearly explains how Satan uses temptation to make us fall. What I like the most is the fact that he uses God's Word, the Bible, as the basis for his explanation of temptation and the solution for overcoming it.

Jonathan Konnerup
Missions Director BBFI

I appreciate Dan Morris' book on this needful topic for several reasons, not the least of which is the author's own decades of faithfulness in the Lord's work. Those serving on the front lines of spiritual battle – as this author has done as a missionary for over a quarter of a century – know firsthand the onslaught of Satan and the need for biblical strategies to live in victory. In this book, you will find a detailed, thorough study of both.

Dr. Paul Chappell
Sr. Pastor Lancaster Baptist Church, President West Coast Baptist College

From early college days forty years ago, I have known Dr. Daniel Morris. He was a very conscientious student, well focused in life. During the past forty years, he has been extremely dedicated, and God has given him many successful ministries.

Dr. Morris writes from his knowledge of the Word of God and his experience in teaching. You will be blessed, inspired, and determined to do a greater work for the Lord as you read his writings.

M. Jack Baskin
Pastor and Mission Consultant

Understanding
& *OVERCOMING*
Temptation

Understanding
& OVERCOMING
Temptation

Protect Yourself from Temptation's Traps

Dr. James Daniel Morris

Printed in the United States of America
Aneko Press – *Our Readers Matter*™
www.anekopress.com
Aneko Press, Life Sentence Publishing, and our logos are trademarks of
Life Sentence Publishing, Inc.
P.O. Box 652
Abbotsford, WI 54405
RELIGION / Christian Life / Spiritual Warfare
Paperback ISBN: 978-1-62245-236-1
Ebook ISBN: 978-1-62245-237-8
10 9 8 7 6 5 4 3 2 1
This book is available from www.amazon.com, Barnes & Noble, and your local bookstore.
Share this book on Facebook:

Contents

SECTION 1

Understanding Temptation

CHAPTER 1

The Damage of Sin

How we are hurt by the shame of sin. What suffering comes upon us when precious relationships are cooled or even destroyed by someone doing wrong. Building an honorable reputation is difficult, but losing it is so easy. How many parents have agonized over children following destructive paths, especially if they know they contributed to the situation with their own failures?

Can we avoid this hurt and shame? Is there an answer? Can we enjoy the benefits of what is good, right, and wise, not only in our own life experiences but also in the lives of loved ones? Answering these questions requires understanding what causes these destructive failures.

"Why did I do that?" I ask. That question is normally an expression of despair. The problem is we don't really seek the answer. This book will attempt to find clear answers to that question and, through understanding the forces and processes involved, provide practical steps that will give hope of avoiding further damage and allow enjoyment of the life God wants his children to experience.

When a wrong is committed in society, officers of the law begin an investigation to find out who was the perpetrator. They trace the crime back to the guilty party by observing the telltale evidences. What happened? How did this come about? We ask the same questions in our own experiences, so we also must observe the elements involved in order to understand the problem. Then, we can take steps to achieve the peace we long for.

CHAPTER 2

The Force of Temptation

Again, consider that question, why did I do that? I know I have the potential to sin, but why did I actually commit that wrong? Something initiated a process in my life that resulted in a sinful thought or action. Temptation is what we call this original force that initiates a process resulting in sin. Knowing that is nothing new. But why is this force so effective? Why does it defeat us time after time? Why do we relate so well to Oscar Wilde's statement, "I can resist anything except temptation"?[1] It is not enough to know about the force of temptation. Our hope of victory depends upon understanding this force, how it works, and what our reactions should be. This understanding is equally important in our relationships with others, because our reactions to their failures affect our lives as much as do our own failures.

The subject of this book is important. We all experience this force every day. The damages are innumerable, ranging from being overweight to the destruction of lives, marriages, churches, and nations. Every life has been touched by this force in one way or another.

Much is made over destructive forces that damage and destroy lives, such as physical abuse and additions. It is amazing that so little attention is given to the destructive force of temptation. When attention is given to this harmful power, it is usually with great hypocrisy, condemned in one particular

---

1   Jerry and Kirsti Newcombe, *A Way of Escape* (Nashville: Broadman and Holman, 1999).

area and condoned or defended in another. All of this contributes to the universal damage and suffering that the power of temptation brings upon mankind.

To understand temptation, we must begin by defining the word. *Webster's Dictionary of 1828* provides one of the clearest and most exhaustive definitions that any dictionary has ever offered. Its definition of temptation is as follows:

> "**Temptation, *n.*** The act of tempting; enticement to evil by arguments, by flattery, or by the offer of some real or apparent good. [. . .] 2. Solicitation of the passions; enticements to evil proceeding from the prospect of pleasure or advantage. 3. The state of being tempted or enticed to evil. When by human weakness you are led into temptation, resort to prayer for relief. 4. Trial. [. . .] 5. That which is presented to the mind as an inducement to evil. Dare to be great without a guilty crown. View it, and lay the bright *temptation* down. *Dryden.* 6. In *colloquial language*, an allurement to anything indifferent, or even good."[2]

Careful examination of this definition reveals that temptation has to do with two different concepts: the enticement of sin and the enticement of behavior that isn't necessarily sin. This study will deal entirely with the concept of enticement to wrong behavior or sin.

Temptation that is Not Sin

It may seem difficult to distinguish between temptation and sin. This was one of the experiences that tormented Pilgrim in John Bunyan's *The Pilgrim's Progress.* As he walked through the Valley of the Shadow of Death, he said,

2   Noah Webster, *American Dictionary of the English Language*, 1st ed. (Anaheim: Foundation for American Christian Education, 1967).

"One thing I would not let slip; I took notice that now poor Christian was so confounded that he did not know his own voice. And thus I perceived it: just when he was come over against the mouth of the burning Pit one of the wicked ones got behind him and stept up softly to him; and whisperingly suggested many grievous blasphemies to him – which he verily thought had proceeded from his own mind. This put Christian more to it than anything that he met with before, even to think that he should now blaspheme Him that he loved so much before! Yet if he could have helped it, he would not have done it; but he had not the discretion neither to stop his ears, nor to know from whence those blasphemies came."[3]

This is a picture of how temptation in the mind can seem like sin and yet not be sin. Up to this point, the evil is Satan's. The evil thoughts are his devices that are sown in the mind of a person in a way that they appear to be his own. This can torment him as it did Christian who couldn't understand how he could have such blasphemous thoughts. Satan's thoughts can tempt us, but as long as these thoughts or feelings are rejected, sin has not been committed.

Charles Stanley says, "We serve a just and righteous God. He will not hold us responsible for things over which we have no control. He knows Satan is working full-time to flood our ears, eyes, and minds with things that will sidetrack us. God will not judge us for those evil thoughts that dart through our minds, not even for those longings and desires that often accompany certain thoughts. On the contrary, he sent his son to enable us to successfully deal with the onslaught of temptation. Temptation is not a sin; it is simply Satan's attempt to make us fall."[4]

---

3   John Bunyan, *The Pilgrim's Progress*, 1973 Ed. (Grand Rapids: Zondervan 1967).
4   Charles Stanley, *Winning the War Within* (Nashville: Thomas Nelson Publishers 1977), 163.

Temptation that Leads to Sin

However, if the thoughts or feelings are accepted and acted upon, either mentally or openly, God's will is not obeyed, and sin is committed. Sin is, therefore, an act of willfulness regarding temptation. Man's will is what makes the difference and the "prize" that the Devil seeks to win (we shall study this in greater depth later).

Many forces are at work in the process of temptation. If we can shed light on these forces and achieve a clear understanding of what is going on in this process, we will have a greater hope of overcoming this destructive force in our lives.

CHAPTER 3

The Weakness of the Flesh

When Adam and Eve were tempted in the garden, they were pure and innocent of heart with no moral weakness. Their weakness was not based on wrong in their lives but rather on the simple human quality of curiosity and the capability of getting their minds off God and his Word. They used their God-given ability to choose according to their own free will. Even though they were sinless until the fall, their reasoning was wrong, and they chose what God had forbidden.

In this age of fallen man, human weaknesses have multiplied due to the corruption of sin in man's body and soul. Although many Christians think of the flesh as being very strong and difficult to control, the biblical view is that *the flesh is weak.*[5] The human viewpoint of a strong fleshly nature seems to be based on the tendency to focus upon the power of evil. Satan uses this nonbiblical viewpoint to continue his deceitful work and cause man to despair in the struggle against the flesh and more easily surrender to its domination.

God's viewpoint, on the other hand, sees the flesh as weak and incapable of continuing in good. This viewpoint results in the emphasis of man's need of spiritual power and utter dependence upon faith, which is how he experiences this power. If one can see the flesh as God sees it, he will tend to recognize the reality of his weak nature and look to Christ for the power to overcome.

As we can see here, this difference in viewpoint is not a

---

5   Mark 14:38.

matter of semantics but rather a crucial element in experiencing victory over temptation. The common feeling of despair and failure should become a wake-up call to the fact that one is looking at the struggle from man's point of view and not from God's. This knowledge can enable a person to realize what is happening and trigger a change of viewpoint that is foundational to overcoming temptation.

What is the Flesh?

Having established the importance of the correct viewpoint concerning the flesh, we can begin to analyze this weakness of fallen man. When the Bible speaks of the flesh, it refers to all that man is that is not changed by the new birth of the spirit. The spirit of man is regenerated and becomes one with the *divine nature* of God.[6] It is, therefore, completely apart from the flesh. The soul and body, however, are not totally renewed. The mind is still full of erroneous thoughts, attitudes, and conclusions that must experience a *renewing*.[7] The emotions are still conformed to these wrong thoughts, attitudes, and conclusions of the mind, and the will is mostly dominated by these thoughts and emotions.

The body is also not renewed. The glorification of the body, *raised in incorruption,* is a hope based upon the promised resurrection in the end times.[8] At present, the body tires, ages, hurts, and suffers hunger, thirst, and sickness. It has a constant demand to fulfill its natural appetites and desires for comforts.

Curiosity

Having described what the flesh is, the first factor to analyze is the relationship between normal curiosity and temptation.

---

6   2 Peter 1:4.

7   Romans 12:2.

8   1 Corinthians 15:42-44.

Again, a good dictionary definition of this word is useful as a starting point. The *Webster's Dictionary of 1828* gives this primary definition of curiosity:

> "**Curiosity** 1. A strong desire to see something novel, or to discover something unknown, either by research or inquiry; a desire to gratify the senses with a sight of what is new or unusual, or to gratify the mind with new discoveries; inquisitiveness. A man's curiosity leads him to view the ruins of Balbec, to investigate the origin of Homer, to discover the component parts of a mineral, or the motives of another's actions."

In other words, the primary concept of curiosity relates to an innate human desire to know or experience something new or unknown. This God-given desire has proven useful and is the root cause of most inventions, discoveries, and human progress that man has achieved. In this sense, curiosity is good and helpful. This desire for understanding is a primary reason that Christians seek to be closer to God and is much of the reason for this book.

Many non-Christians are initially attracted to God out of curiosity. Curiosity is not something to be stifled or inhibited. However, as in the case of all natural instincts or emotions, curiosity can also be used out of the context of good. For this reason, the apostle Paul exhorted the Christians at Rome to be *wise unto that which is good and a simple concerning evil.*[9]

If curiosity is focused on areas in which disobedience can occur, it can become the primary part of the process of temptation. Eve probably did not arrive by coincidence at the place where the tree of the knowledge of good and evil was growing. Having heard God's warning about the consequences of

---

9   Romans 16:19.

eating the forbidden fruit, her natural curiosity probably led her to want to see it with her own eyes. With Satan's deceit, that curiosity led to the lust of the eyes, the lust of the flesh, and the pride of life that, in turn, led to sin and death.

We see then that while curiosity should not be stifled, it must be controlled and properly directed. As children, we were admonished by parents and schoolteachers that "curiosity killed the cat." This old saying was their way of expressing the need for controlling curiosity. If the proper discipline of natural curiosity is exercised and achieved, temptation will decrease.

This need to discipline curiosity will vary in different people for various reasons. First, the actual innate quality of curiosity varies in strength in each individual and has to do with temperament. Because many factors are involved, no set rules can be established, but tendencies can be observed and proven useful in the pursuit of proper control of curiosity. For instance, the adventurous spirit of the sanguine temperament tends to experience a greater degree of inborn curiosity, whereas the more tranquil and satisfied spirit of the phlegmatic usually experiences a lesser degree. The tendency of the melancholy to be a deep thinker coincides with a greater degree of curiosity, while the choleric's tendency to be practical with known "tools for achievement" will usually show a lesser degree of curiosity. Even though everyone needs to control their curiosity, the sanguine and melancholy need to understand the greater concern they must have, due to the greater strength of curiosity natural for someone of their temperament.

A similar innate difference exists between the sexes. The "trailblazer" instinct is more common in the male and tends to go along with a greater degree of curiosity than the basic security-oriented instinct that is almost universal in the female. Most obviously, the male instinct of sexual attraction through visual stimulation also coincides with a greater experience of natural curiosity about the body than the female experiences. This will be the most common area in which curiosity is related to temptation and will be discussed at length later in this book. Interesting results might also be found in a thorough study of curiosity in relation to other innate differences such as race or even age.

As numerous as innate differences between individuals may be, there are likely even more "developed" differences. These "developed" differences result in varying degrees of curiosity about particular interests the person may have. During the development of an individual's personality, character, and education, certain experiences will arouse a particular interest in something. This interest will, in turn, produce a greater level of curiosity about that subject than about other areas of life. These interests can vary from food to physics.

Sometimes a person's developed interest is due to greater exposure to a specific activity, as in the case of children following parents in work and hobbies. Many times the interest is strengthened by an experience of achievement and the sense of self-value and fulfillment that goes with it. A compliment or prize can be the initial experience that creates a lifelong interest. This includes all areas of education and experience. The physical sciences of biology, geology, or astronomy will excite curiosity differently in people, due to exposure or positive experience in addition to the individual's level of innate curiosity. Others will become more curious about the social sciences of humanity, history, or philosophy. While some will develop a desire to know more about how things are manufactured, others will be curious about how things work in operation.

What does this have to do with temptation? More than we can imagine. Just as exposure to pleasing experiences can result in greater interest in positive and productive areas of life, this exposure can also result in interest in negative and destructive areas of life. This may be a personal exposure to the experience of someone else. The temptation to try drugs is increased by the exposure to friends who use drugs and appear popular. Curiosity may cause the mind to relate the popularity of a person to the drug use. If not popularity, the apparent excitement or testimony of good feelings can excite the curiosity. Exposure to pornography or indecency will result in greater degrees of curiosity about immorality. Conversations heard with certain "friends" or exposure to magazines and television programs will produce an increased level of curiosity about these destructive forces. The degree of exposure will in part determine the degree of curiosity that will become a part of the process of temptation.

School systems that promote sex education in increasingly lower grade levels either naively ignore or deliberately deny this destructive result of children being exposed to sexuality. Educators believe that this early exposure will result in an awareness and maturity that will allow them to make proper decisions. In reality, because of the educator's own willful ignorance of the forces of curiosity and temptation, the opposite effect is experienced. The increased exposure to the subject of sex increases their curiosity and results in abnormal temptation at ages in which sex would not normally be an interest. Combine the natural lack of maturity and discipline of a young child with the void of accompanying instruction about moral right and wrong, and the result is an overwhelming pressure of temptation that can initiate a process of moral failure for a lifetime. Parents and Christians, especially in education, must prepare themselves with an understanding of these forces and an ability to express them professionally and boldly, in order to counteract the foolish philosophy of thinking something positive will result from sex education in school at early ages or without moral guidelines.

Other factors also contribute to the existence of curiosity or the lack thereof. The first factor is the rule that the satisfaction of curiosity varies according to physical possibilities. This, in turn, affects the degree of temptation to satisfy that curiosity. Take into consideration again that our basic definition of curiosity is a desire to know something new or unknown. As I write today, I am sitting in a motel room looking at a piece of furniture with two drawers. Curiosity will make me wonder what is in the drawers. I can satisfy that curiosity quite easily because, for today, this is my motel room, and I have a right to open those drawers. Every other motel room has similar drawers, but they do not arouse my curiosity as much for the simple reason that the possibility of inspecting them is much lower. There is also a wall before me, but I have very little curiosity about what is inside the wall, in part because of the lack of the possibility of finding out. This possibility factor can also depend on my rights in relation to an object or some other reason that facilitates the satisfaction.

Again we can see how this factor is important when we think about how Eve made it easier to satisfy her curiosity and give in to temptation by going to the area of the forbidden tree. Much of the reason less immorality existed in the past is simply that the possibilities did not exist as extensively as today. Movies were decent, indecency on TV was unheard of, and perverse literature was unacceptable in the open.

The consumption of fattening foods and the use of drugs has also been proportional to the ease with which they can be obtained. Therefore, the control of curiosity and resulting temptation will also depend upon limiting the possibilities. The seductiveness of clothing is related to this possibility factor. A miniskirt may be less revealing than a conservative swimming suit, yet the miniskirt is more seductive because it has less defined or fixed boundaries, while the swimsuit has more defined or fixed boundaries. The possibility of change in boundaries is what makes the miniskirt more seductive. Understanding this principle will eliminate many excuses for seductive dress behavior.

Even advances in science illustrate the dependence of curiosity upon possibilities. When the steam engine was invented, the resulting serious curiosity was about how it could be used and improved. Space travel may have been a fantasy at that time but did not become a subject of active curiosity. However, as progress made space travel more and more possible, it became a true object of curiosity and is being progressively more satisfied.

If we relate this principle again to moral standards of right and wrong, we see that as a vice, such as smoking, drinking, drugs, indecency, or immoral behavior, becomes more possible to practice, a result will be increased interest, curiosity, and temptation.

Another factor to consider is the rule that the degree of curiosity varies proportionally to the degree of the unknown vs. the known. Take again the drawers I mentioned. If they were slightly opened and I could see some of the inside, my curiosity would decrease. The more the drawer is opened, the less there is that is unknown, and thus my curiosity is lessened. If, however, I could see part of an unknown object, my curiosity might increase. The more unknown elements in the situation, the more curiosity there may be.

At this point another factor comes into play, which is the rule that curiosity will either grow or diminish according to experience. Since I have seen the contents of many motel room drawers, the factor of the unknown decreases, and with it, my degree of curiosity. Also, if an object is partially visible, my curiosity may either increase or decrease, depending on my previous experience. If I had experience with the object of temptation, I might imagine the possibility of another similar experience, and my curiosity will increase. On the other hand, if my previous experience did not involve this object, that knowledge will result in a lack of curiosity. Experience can be triggered in many ways. An ugly, round rock may be uninteresting to most people, but if one has the experience of having seen the beautiful crystals inside a geode, the round rock may excite great curiosity. Experience may relate to anything of interest from food to finances, from caves to caskets.

Unfortunately, this factor also has a moral side. Innocence, or as Paul said, being *simple to evil*,[10] is precisely a lack of experience in sinful matters. When this innocence is lost due to experience, a greater awakening of curiosity occurs in relation to immoral practices. "You don't miss what you've never had" is an old but true principle. Sometimes experience comes intentionally in a gradual process (to be discussed at length later). Experience can also come in an unintentional manner. Whatever the manner, however, the result will be the same. A degree of innocence will be lost, and a degree of curiosity will come into play that was not previously experienced. This new curiosity will produce temptation if the matter concerns a moral wrong. Thus we see the importance of Paul's admonition to be wise to good and simple to evil.

The last factor relates to the rule that says reward for an activity produces a desire to repeat the activity and be further rewarded. Curiosity always pertains to some unknown element. In the case of the reward factor, the unknown may be either the activity or the reward. In other words, it may have to do with an imagined or possible activity that produces a known reward or a known activity that may produce an imagined reward. Satan used this against Eve. He placed into her mind the thought that a reward of being wise like God would result from a known activity, eating the fruit. The reward was not only imagined, it was entirely false. Herein lies another danger of

10   Romans 16:19.

curiosity. Often, the supposed benefits of the activity are temporal, superficial, or entirely false. The reward can be a lie, or it can be a pleasure that results in disastrous and unintended consequences.

The degree of attraction will depend upon the value of the reward. This value is not inherent but rather a subjective value in the individual's mind. To one person, self-esteem may be a much greater reward than money or even health. To another, adventure may produce the great sense of reward. Whatever the case, the greater the subjective value of the reward, the greater the curiosity about the activity.

After considering the various factors involved in the concept of curiosity, we can simplify them as a formula and see how it can be dealt with. Consider the following:

Degree of Curiosity about _____ =

(drugs, alcohol, sex, pornography, occult, religions, gangs, fame, power, robbery, etc.)

Factor Scale 0 – 10

_____ Innate Strength
_____ Developed Interests
_____ Possibilities
_____ Known – Unknown
_____ Experience
_____ Reward

Total Possible 0 – 60

Scale of 0 to 60 = The Strength of Curiosity that Can Lead to Temptation

0---------10---------20---------30---------40---------5---------60

If a person fills in the blanks with an honest ranking of 0 to 10 in the six areas related to his curiosity level about the particular subject, the strength of his curiosity becomes apparent and shows how susceptible he is to temptation. He can then make adjustments to minimize or maximize each area. This will be discussed in detail later.

Obsession

Having discussed the factor of curiosity in relation to temptation, we must also deal with obsession. Webster defines obsession as: "The act of besieging; the first attack of Satan antecedent to possession; the state of being ruled by one idea or desire; a ruling idea, a mania. [. . .]"[11]

Obsession and curiosity are similar in how they are first experienced inwardly and then lead to outward actions and behavior. The fact that these forces can be directed toward right behavior as well as wrong is another similarity. However, as is apparent from the definition, obsession differs from curiosity in that it is not an innate force but rather a drive that is produced by an outside influence. This influence is the work of Satan himself, even though in many cases he may use another person as the direct influence.

Amnon, the firstborn son of David, is a clear example of the force of obsession that dominates the will. He became obsessed with lust for his half-sister Tamar. This obsession enslaved him mentally to the point that all of life centered upon its fulfillment. His spiritual, emotional, and even physical state were affected and dominated by this force. The result was an irrational way of thinking that was blind to all consequences, and finally, actions that destroyed his life and the lives of others.

John Owen describes this aspect of temptation, saying: "One temptation—whether it is a lust, or a warped attitude, or anything else—becomes one's whole obsession. We might cite the carnal fear of Peter, the pride of Hezekiah, the covetousness of Achan, the uncleanness of David, the worldliness of Demas, or the ambition of Diotrephes. We do not know the pride, fury,

---

11   Webster, *American Dictionary.*

and madness of a wrong deed until we face a suitable temptation. How tragic is the life of someone whose mind is darkened, whose affections are entangled, and whose lusts are enflamed, so that his defenses break down. What hope remains for him?"[12]

The potential for great destruction makes this a serious matter, one that should be understood and stopped. As in the case of curiosity, if the process of obsession can be broken down and understood, it can also be prevented or detained and undone.

Normally, obsession begins with curiosity. The factors of curiosity work together to produce an interest in some activity. At this point, Satan begins to bombard the mind with thoughts and suggestions to intensify one's focus upon the object of his curiosity. The influences of other people are used to continue developing this intensity of focus and interest. Certainly demonic activity can be involved under Satan's direction. If one is unaware of this process and shows little resistance, his focus narrows and centers more and more upon the object of obsession, until he is enslaved mentally, emotionally, and physically. At this point, his will is dominated, and Satan's destructive purposes are carried out.

The basic steps in the process of developing an obsession are therefore: (1) curiosity, (2) interest, (3) narrowing focus, and 4) slavery. However, there are at least two very different directions of behavior that can result in this process. This difference develops in the second step of the process, which is the development of an interest. The factor that causes the difference is the difficulty or lack of difficulty in fulfilling this interest.

First, let us consider the direction of behavior that results when the object of this intense interest is easy to obtain and the desire is therefore fulfilled. As the process continues into step three, the narrowing of focus and attention upon the object or

---

12 John Owen, *Sin and Temptation*, ed. Dr. James M. Houston (Minneapolis: Bethany House Publishers, 1996), 115.

activity, what occurs is a continual repetition of the activity or desire. In the final step, slavery, the outward behavior is a mental, physical, or emotional addiction to the object or activity. Some common obsessions that result in physical addiction are drugs, alcohol, or other substances that can be abused, as well as the consumption of legitimate foods to the point of gluttony and obesity. Emotional addiction can result in areas of pornography and other sensual activities. Mental addiction is also possible, resulting in a life of fantasies and foolish philosophies.

Another direction of behavior can result when the object of intense interest is difficult or impossible to achieve. In the process of normal curiosity, we have seen how this will produce a decrease in interest. The process of obsession is different, however. Through the work of outside influences directed by Satan, the intensity of interest will multiply. As this develops into the narrowing focus of step three, the intensity of interest combined with the difficulty of fulfillment results in a growing, tormenting desire, as was the case in the life of Amnon. Finally, as the slavery of step four comes to pass, the outside behavior becomes an irrational mental and emotional state due to the fact that consequences and reality have been obscured. At this point, a terrible potential for any type of destructive or deadly behavior exists.

Other Causes of Weakness

All that is not renewed by regeneration is considered *natural man,* the *old man,* or the term we will use, the *flesh.* Even in a healthy, contented state, the flesh is weak. This weakness is further amplified to an even greater degree of weakness when there is a self-centered state of mind in times of suffering or some lack of natural needs. In fact, one of Jesus' most direct exhortations in regards to temptation occurred when his disciples slept while he was praying in the garden of Gethsemane.[13] Their bodies and minds were weary, possibly due to the stress of the circumstances, journeys, discomforts, and natural need of sleep. Their wills were weakened more than normal.

Loneliness also adds to the natural weakness of the flesh. The lack of fulfillment of the natural desire for company and acceptance has led many to sacrifice their standards and obedience to achieve some relief. In some cases, it is the desire for relief from sickness and pain that makes a man susceptible to the temptation to take circumstances into his own hands, sacrifice obedience to the Lord, and seek relief in some incorrect way. Sometimes defeat is so emotionally painful that relief from the feeling is sought at any cost. Rejection is another feeling that makes man more susceptible to temptation, leading him to seek relief even against his knowledge of what is right.

It must be mentioned, however, that these factors that have the potential to add to the weakness of the flesh also have the potential to produce the opposite effect, the strengthening of the spirit. Paul's suffering produced a conclusion that *when I am weak then am I strong.*[14]

This spiritual strengthening through suffering and trials results when a person "flees to Christ" for help instead of relying upon himself. I once heard a woman say that trials can either coax a person away from Christ or drive him closer. This illustrates what this book is attempting – to produce an understanding of the process of temptation so the will can be directed to prevent that which can be avoided and the spiritual strength to resist and overcome temptation can be found.

The Comfort Zone

Strange as it may seem, although pain and trials may add to

---

13   Luke 22:46.
14   2 Corinthians 12:10.

the natural weakness of the flesh, the experiences of victory, achievements, or comforts can also have the same effect. God warned Israel to beware of this danger, saying:

> And it shall be, when the LORD thy God shall have brought thee into the land which he sware unto thy fathers, to Abraham, to Isaac, and to Jacob, to give thee great and goodly cities, which thou buildedst not, And houses full of all good things, which thou filledst not, and wells digged, which thou diggedst not, vineyards and olive trees, which thou plantedst not; when thou shalt have eaten and be full; Then beware lest thou forget the LORD, which brought thee forth out of the land of Egypt, from the house of bondage. (Deuteronomy 6:10-12)

Sadly, the exhortation was not passed down from parents to children, and in Judges 2:10 we find that the danger became reality.

> And also all that generation were gathered unto their fathers: and there arose another generation after them, which knew not the LORD, nor yet the works which he had done for Israel.

When a person is struggling spiritually, emotionally, mentally, and physically, his need for God's power and blessing is unmistakable. This produces the elements of spiritual strength – humility before God, close fellowship with him, and trust in his power. However, all too often when a person achieves his purpose and the struggle is ended, the sense of great need for God diminishes. The need is no longer objectively related to a cause. The mind is distracted from fellowship with God to the joy of victory. One finds himself in the comfort zone.

Charles Stanley describes this change in our sense of needing God, saying: "It is ironic that we want Him to come rushing into our lives when things get out of our control, when there is a death or an emergency. At those times we are more than willing to admit our inadequacy and our dependence on Him. But as soon as things return to normal, as soon as life gets "easy" again, we are afraid to hand it all over to Him. Think about it. If God can be trusted when we are most vulnerable and helpless, can He not be trusted in the times when things are going smoothly?"[15]

In the time of ease, a person's own strength appears to be sufficient to meet his needs. His dependence upon God becomes vague and theoretical, even if recognized verbally and openly. It doesn't seem real, or it is simply not occupying the mind. Small obstacles or irritations that were insignificant during the time of great struggle now become bothersome, and boredom may set in due to the lack of definite daily purpose.

All of this produces a sense of self-dependence, self-centeredness, and a desire for self-fulfillment, which adds to the natural weakness of the flesh and increases one's susceptibility to temptation. C. S. Lewis's demon, Screwtape, expressed his delight with this situation when teaching his young demon nephew:

> "Prosperity knits a man to the World. He feels that he is 'finding his place in it'; while really it is finding its place in him. His increasing reputation, his widening circle of acquaintances, his sense of importance, the growing pressure of absorbing and agreeable work, build up in him a sense of being really at home in earth which is just what we want."[16]

Sometimes the result is the temptation to petty wrongs such as contentiousness, unjust judgment, or punishments. This is very common in the United States among Christians and ministers whose lives and ministries are more situated in the comfort zone than Christians and ministers in other countries who struggle for basic survival, health, and freedom. These Christians cannot

---

15   Stanley, *Winning the War Within*, 175
16   C. S. Lewis, *The Screwtape Letters* (Uhrichsville: Barbour and Company), 143.

comprehend why Christians in the United States or other developed countries can irritate others of their own faith or church over trite or nonessential issues.

The added weakness of the comfort zone sometimes produces a lack of spiritual vigilance that Satan can use to set a trap and bring about a major fall. This is what happened with King David. While he was fighting life-threatening battles with the Philistines and later running for his life from Saul, he continually sought God's help and depended upon him. Lust was not a major struggle in those times. But when he was king and able to stay home and let others fight the battles, his mind was not drawn to God with the former sense of dependence. Satan set him up for his great fall with Bathsheba and, subsequently, the murder of her husband.

The danger of this "spiritual sleep" is described in *The Pilgrim's Progress*. Christian and Hopeful were warned of the dangers of drowsiness in the "Enchanted Ground."

> "I saw then in my dream, that they went till they came into a certain country, whose air naturally tended to make one drowsy, if he came a stranger into it. And here Hopeful began to be very dull and heavy of sleep; Wherefore he said unto Christian, 'I do now begin to grow so drowsy, that I can scarcely hold up mine eyes; let us lie down here and take one nap.'
>
> *Chr.* 'By no means, said the other; lest sleeping, we never awake more.'
>
> *Hope.* Why, my brother, sleep is sweet to the labouring man; we may be refreshed if we take a nap.
>
> *Chr.* Do not you remember that one of the shepherds bid us beware of the Enchanted Ground? He meant by that that we should beware of sleeping;

Wherefore let us not sleep as others, but let us watch and be sober (1 Thess. 5:6).

Hope. I acknowledge myself in a fault; and had I been here alone, I had, by sleeping, run the danger of death. I see it is true that the Wise Man saith, *'Two are better than one'* (Eccles. 4:9). Hitherto hath thy company been my mercy; and thou shalt have a good reward for thy labour."[17]

Overconfidence

Another much related factor that adds to the natural weakness of the flesh is overconfidence. John Owen spoke of this factor , saying: "In ourselves, we are weakness itself. We have no strength, no power to withstand. Self-confidence produces a large part of our weakness, as it did with Peter. He who boasts that he can do anything, can in fact do nothing as he should. This is the worst form of weakness, similar to treachery."[18]

"Peter learned later to know his own heart. When he had received more of the Holy Spirit and power, he acted with much less self-confidence. He saw that it was best that others should have less confidence as well. Thus he persuades all men *to pass the time of your sojourning here in fear* (1 Peter 1:17). If they had overconfidence, he knew they would fall as he had fallen."[19]

Athletes and coaches are aware of this weakness. Many upsets have occurred in games due to overconfidence. A strong, highly favored athlete or team is aware of their own superior capability and the likelihood of defeating their weaker opponent. This knowledge, however, affects their sense of need in regards to the planning of strategy, training, and actual intensity of their competitive performance in the match-up. The opponent, on

---

17   Bunyan, *Pilgrim's Progress,* 126.
18   Owen, *Sin and Temptation,* 111.
19   Owen, *Sin and Temptation,* 130.

the other hand, has a strong sense of need regarding everything necessary to compete. The intensity of their wills can often overcome their overconfident opponent.

This same danger can occur when a person has experienced an obvious period of spiritual growth and victory. Just as the apostle Paul expressed a sense in which *when I am weak then am I strong*, there is also a sense in which when I am strong, then am I weak. After spiritual growth or victory there is a tendency to feel strong. As in the case of the comfort zone, this feeling of strength dulls the sense of total need for dependence upon the Lord, which is indispensable for true spiritual strength. The feeling of strength after a victory is, therefore, a weakness that again adds to the natural weakness of the flesh and increases susceptibility to temptation. This feeling is a form of pride and *pride cometh before a fall*.[20] Paul also exhorted the Corinthians about this danger, warning, *he who thinketh he standeth take heed lest he fall*.[21]

Jerry and Kirsti Newcombe state, "We are told to work out our salvation with fear and trembling, and we should never think that *we* are immune to temptation or that *we* could never fall. To think that way makes us prime candidates for the arrows of the evil one."[22]

When a man *thinketh he standeth*, or in other words, trusts that he is strong in himself and need not worry about a lack of stability to resist temptation, he is actually in particular danger of falling. The illusion of human strength hinders wisdom and good judgment. Sound thinking is based upon a realistic view of the danger of temptation, the weakness of the flesh, and self-confidence in place of absolute dependence upon God's power and strength.

---

20   Proverbs 16:18.
21   1 Corinthians 10:12.
22   Newcombe, *A Way of Escape,* 4.

Some of the greatest men in history fell into this deceitful trap. David's pride caused him to take a census of his armies. When there were no more major adversaries forcing him to rely on God's power, he became overconfident. So hindered was his clear thinking and judgment, that he ignored both the admonition of Joab and the law of Moses. The consequences were disastrous for his country and personal reputation.

This same trap of overconfidence can be seen in David's son, Solomon. In spite of the divine gift of wisdom he received that made his good judgment known throughout the world, Solomon did not notice how his fame, riches, and glory were setting him up for becoming overconfident. The pitiful end of this great man's life and the division of God's people are testimonies of how dangerous this weakening factor of the flesh can be.[23] Knowing that this danger may follow any planned activity which could result in spiritual growth or victory, Christians would be wise to plan for a time of meditation regarding this weakening factor and focus on the words of Christ that *without me ye can do nothing.*[24]

Age

Different periods of life, age and development are prone to more specific weaknesses. During our youth, sensuality presents an exceptional danger of temptation. Changes in body chemistry increase interest in sexual fulfillment. The lack of maturity and self-control further increase the risk of falling to temptation. If we add to this the youthful desire for acceptance and the tremendous power of peer pressure in a world that promotes promiscuous behavior, the result is greater weakness in this area of temptation than is normal in other stages of life. Observe how Job apparently refers to this experience when he said that it was

---

23   Nehemiah 13:26.
24   John 15:5.

not just, at that period of his life, to be judged for *the iniquities of my youth.*[25]

Another consequence of the developmental changes in youth is the tendency to be *lifted up with pride.*[26] The transition between depending upon parents to independence produces many opportunities to satisfy the desire to do things "my own way." This new feeling of power is as gratifying as any vice and adds to the natural weakness of the flesh in the areas of pride and self-centeredness. Because of little practical experience, young people rely upon untested but seemingly rational ideas. They struggle to recognize their limitations and tend to jump to conclusions. Advice, counsel, or correction feel like a threat to their new and satisfying sense of independence and is easily rejected. Again, the level of natural weakness is increased by these tendencies.

Other seasons of life carry particular dangers. For instance, when a man reaches middle age and finds his dreams have not been fulfilled, and he may have even experienced setbacks or defeats, discouragement may result. Life's circumstances, work, and even family experiences can create an increasing sense of unfulfillment and drudgery. During this period, anything that gives the sense of fun, happiness, or self-value seems to be a welcome escape from the normal drudgery of life. Under these circumstances, anything or anyone who causes the sense of self-worth and acceptance that is so desirable but elusive becomes a special attraction. Various things can satisfy this longing for something gratifying. The pleasure of foods, drinks, and sweets becomes significant and can lead to obesity or addictions. Peer pressure regains its strength at this time of life and brings about changes in behavior, interests, and even standards of right and wrong. Many ministries have experienced drastic changes in

---

25   Job 13:26.
26   1Timothy 3:6.

strategy, standards, music, and fellowship due to this longing in the life of a middle-aged pastor. One of the most dangerous and destructive situations is the greater susceptibility to moral temptation due to the great desire for acceptance and admiration, aside from the temptation to physical pleasure. Most affairs begin with the sense of gratification felt when admired by someone of the opposite sex. The longing of this age can be so strong that even family, friends, and reputation may be sacrificed. This is tragic, because such fulfillment is almost always temporary and superficial. By the time one wakes up to reality, restoration is impossible.

Gradual Process

Over the years, I have heard many preachers and youth leaders use an illustration of how a frog reacts differently to abrupt changes in temperature as opposed to gradual changes. I have not substantiated this experiment, but the illustration is worthwhile whatever the case. It is told that if a frog is placed into a pan of hot water, it will frantically jump out to escape. However, since a frog is cold-blooded and adapts to temperature changes, if the frog is placed into a pan of water that has the temperature equal to that of a frog's present state and the water is gradually warmed, the frog will not notice the change and will die from the heat without knowing what is happening.

This illustration is used to warn people of another weakness of the flesh – its tendency to adjust to attitudes or activities that are wrong without noticing the degree of change that has occurred. An abrupt change would have caused a severe conflict with the conscience. If the change is gradual, the same change can occur and be completely acceptable.

Jerry and Kirsti Newcombe warn, "Backsliding, quite often, can be a gradual thing. Even the term *slide* doesn't necessarily denote a quick fall. It implies a slow move down a hill, for instance. At least it may begin in a slow way. But once the speed picks up, the slider can move at a quick pace."

At the end of the same paragraph they cite C.S. Lewis, who said, "The safest [surest] road to Hell is the gradual one—the gentle slope, soft under foot, without sudden turnings, without milestones, without signposts."[27]

This principle of susceptibility to gradual temptation is yet another factor that adds to the normal weakness of the flesh. Since it has to do with the conscience, it will be covered again with that subject.

Weaknesses Related to Specific Parts of the Flesh

Having analyzed the subject of the weakness of the flesh, we can now apply it to the specific parts of the flesh. As we have stated, the flesh is everything about man that was not regenerated – in other words, the soul and body. The complexity of the soul and its relation to the body is probably far greater than we can know. However, it is useful to consider the three elements into which the soul is classed by most Christian writers – the mind, emotions, and will.

The Mind

The mind is the part of the soul that has the ability to reason, learn, judge, remember, and imagine. I will discuss the mind's particular weaknesses as part of the flesh, and as a result, its relation to the process of temptation.

Adam and Eve were the only people who ever lived without sin. Before the fall, their minds were pure of any sinful thoughts, attitudes, or conclusions. However, even with such purity of mind, they had the capability of being corrupted by the knowledge of good and of evil. In comparison to God's mind, this constituted the natural weakness of man's mind. This is

---

27   Newcombe, *A Way of Escape*, 4.

an extremely important lesson in relation to temptation. If a pure mind could be tempted and fall into sin, how much more should we be aware of the probability of our fallen minds being led through the process of temptation toward wrong thoughts, attitudes, and conclusions that produce wrong decisions?

John Owen comments on the mind and temptation, saying: "The power of temptation is to darken the mind, so that a person becomes unable to make right judgments about things as he did before entering into temptation."[28] The understanding of this weakness, however, can produce the humble recognition of our total dependence upon God's Word, the mind of Christ, and the guidance of the Holy Spirit that is the key to overcoming temptation.

The fallen mind is weak in regards to temptation in many ways. From childhood, the fallen mind is concerned with the comforts of the body and the good feelings of the emotions. Subconsciously, the mind begins filing information into the memory about circumstances that produce gratifying comforts and feelings and other circumstances that do not gratify. Although a baby may not have reached the age of accountability in regards to sin, he is already forming conclusions, habits, and attitudes that will be used against him by Satan when he does reach the age of accountability.

The most common experience is related to crying. When the baby feels hunger, pain, or fear, his natural reaction is to cry. In time the mind associates crying with the satisfying of his needs and good feelings. Soon, good feelings become the motivation to cry, and the seed of selfishness is sown. As a child grows, his ever-increasing intelligence is used to obtain ever-increasing types of good feelings in ever more creative ways. Dishonesty and rebellion sometimes produce good feelings, so the mind may identify dishonesty and rebellion as something good. If not for

28 Owen, *Sin and Temptation*, 114.

positive forces and influences to counteract it, this process can fill a mind with incorrect thoughts, attitudes, and conclusions, and the degree of corruption in the mind will affect the degree of susceptibility to temptation.

While the natural tendency of the mind is to come to conclusions based upon information that makes good feelings and comforts possible, the mind is also constantly exposed to error. Sometimes error can be formed through the natural process of reasoning that is based on a lack of experience, a lack of information, a lack of logic, or prejudice due to attitudes formed beforehand. Other times the error is simply transferred from one person's mind to another's that will accept the information as authoritative, true, or at least "good." Still other error is the result of purposeful deceit and manipulation. The mind, therefore, is extremely susceptible to temptation and is part of the weakness of the flesh.

For this reason, the Scriptures place great emphasis upon the mind. The Bible itself is given by God to prevent or undo erroneous thoughts, attitudes, and conclusions. It establishes truth and defines right and wrong so the mind will have the necessary foundation for correct reasoning and, in turn, for correct decisions. For this reason, David could say, *Thy word have I hid in mine heart that I might not sin against thee.*[29] Actually, the entire 119th Psalm is dedicated to this principle, as is the entire Bible. This principle is at the root of Jesus' teaching to his people that *ye are the light of the world.*[30] Christians are light because they have the knowledge of the truth. That light shines in darkness, meaning other minds are taught the truth by them. For this reason Paul says, *faith cometh by hearing and hearing by the Word of God.*[31]

---

29   Psalm 119:11.
30   Matthew 5:14.
31   Romans 10:17.

God instructs us to be about this business of strengthening our minds with the truth in the earliest stages of life. *Train up a child in the way he should go and when he is old he will not depart from it* (Proverbs 22:6). The first part of Deuteronomy 6, including what Christ called the Great Commandment, deals with this responsibility to enlighten the minds of children with truth, and in so doing, protect them from error and temptation. Jesus prayed that the Father would sanctify his disciples by his truth. Most of our spiritual warfare against Satan, the father of lies, has to do with learning and proclaiming truth.

The Emotions

We now come to the second element of the soul – the emotions. Emotions are feelings. Just as the whole spectrum of colors are produced by the three basic colors, in a similar way a myriad of emotions spring from three basic emotions: love, anger, and fear. Before the fall, Adam and Eve were as pure and innocent in their emotions as they were in their minds. Even though they had the potential to experience all three emotions, there was practically nothing in their minds or their circumstances to provoke the feelings of anger and fear. This does not mean that they did not exist, however. There is a positive side to all emotions. Even God in his absolute holiness has expressed his divine anger toward evil. Imagining the emotion of fear in God is more difficult. However, his constant warnings to his people to abstain from evil in order to avoid its consequences and curses demonstrate a concern for his children regarding dangers. This includes the divine element of caution, an emotion that combines both love and fear.

Whatever the case, Adam and Eve probably had no experiences with anger, and fear was probably only related to the Lord's command not to eat of the forbidden fruit. Even in this, the fear of the Lord was lacking. For this reason, we can conclude that the emotion that filled their lives was love. This would be understandable given God's desire for loving fellowship with man, and that love is even greater than faith and hope.[32] This love would be expressed to both God and creation in multiple ways, including affection, desire for well-being, and compassion. Heaven must be similar in this way, which is part of the Christian's blessed hope.

However, as a result of the fall, Satan has corrupted the emotions, and instead of being a joyful blessing, they have the potential to cause great damage and hurt. Anger and fear are now primary emotions, and even love has been degenerated. Due to sinful man's self-consciousness and self-concern, he is dominated by desire for self-fulfilling feelings. Even the mind is directed by feelings, making emotions the single most powerful force over a man's will.

Satan knows God's desire for the heart and love of man. He cannot fathom how great that desire is with God, but he strives to either divert it away from God or substitute it with other destructive emotions. Love can then be directed to self which results in lust, envy, jealousy, distrust, maliciousness, and vengeance. In all their degenerated forms anger and fear can be combined with self-love to complete the scale of wrong, hurtful, and ungodly feelings. These may be as simple as apathy and indifference or as destructive as hate. These emotions may produce behavior as obvious as common selfishness, but they could also be the motive for some religious practices. They might motivate one to act very hospitably, or they might drive one to lawlessness. Even the most heinous crimes can proceed from self-love.

All of this demonstrates once again just how weak the flesh is and how susceptible it is to temptation. This is why we find the greatest men of God, such as David, falling headlong into sin. Even Solomon, with his divine gift of wisdom and discernment, fell prey to the subtle process of temptation.

32   1 Corinthians 13:13.

The Will

The third part of the soul is the will. With the will, man freely decides his course of action in life. The will determines what man is, and this is related to, if not synonymous with, his character. Because the will determines a man's loyalty, faith, and purpose in life, it is the prize for which spiritual forces of good and evil do battle. He who has a man's will has the man. However, God made the will free, so it cannot be directly attacked or dominated. Satan cannot capture man's will by force, and God will not take man's will by force. The will can only be influenced by the rest of his being: Spirit, soul (emotions and mind), and body. God uses man's conscience, which we will study later, through the influences of the Bible, the Holy Spirit, Christians, demonstrations of love, or trials and afflictions to gain man's willing submission, his honor, and his love. Satan uses the weakness of man's flesh, mind, emotions, and body to tempt him to willingly disobey God. In so doing, man submits himself to Satan by loving and honoring his ways of life.

The demon Screwtape describes this difference , saying: "The reason is this. To us a human is primarily food; our aim is the absorption of its will into ours, the increase of our own area of selfhood at its expense. But the obedience which the Enemy [God] demands of men is quite a different thing. One must face the fact that all the talk about his love for men, and His service being perfect freedom, is not (as one would gladly believe) propaganda, but an appalling truth. He really *does* want to fill the universe with a lot of loathsome little replicas of Himself—creatures whose life, on its miniature scale, will be qualitatively like His own, not because He has absorbed them but because their wills freely conform to his."[33]

Although the will is considered a part of the soul, it is unique. It is the neutral "go-between" in relation to the unregenerate flesh

---

33 Lewis, *Screwtape Letters,* 45.

and the regenerate spirit. To perfectly explain this mystery is not possible. If the will is indeed part of the unregenerate soul of man, it is at least uniquely freed from bondage to sin and therefore neutral in essence. The will is not neutral in practice, however. The will is either in submission to God or in disobedience to him. We can conclude that the relation of the will to temptation is, however, entirely indirect.

The Body

Besides the powerful influences of the mind and emotions, the body also influences the will. God designed the body to have certain needs. He made it dependent upon food and water for nourishment and sustenance for its different organisms. In order for this to be fulfilled, he gave the body a natural desire or appetite for food and water. Furthermore, he gave the body a sense of pleasure when these appetites are fulfilled and a sense of displeasure when they are not. In this way, he not only took care of his creation's needs, he also showed his love in providing for his joy.

The same applies to God's desire for man to multiply. He gave the body an appetite for sexual intercourse and made the fulfillment thereof a great pleasure. These appetites, of course, were also given to the bodies of animals for the same natural purposes. Man, however, was created in God's image with intellect, emotions, and will on an entirely different plane from that of all other life. Man was not only given appetites, he was also given order and conscience. He was told to eat and drink of all that was made by God for that purpose, but he was also told not to eat what God did not allow. He was given a wife and through the institution of marriage made to be united with her in one flesh.

Besides these life-sustaining, life-multiplying, and joy-producing appetites, God also gave the body the five senses. Through these five senses, man could respond to his physical environment and experience great joy and pleasure. These appetites and senses of the body were very good; they were a part of the paradise God had prepared for man through his love and goodness.

This also, however, was corrupted in the fall. Natural appetites are now fulfilled out of God's order and in disobedience. Charles Stanley says, "We forget that although God gave us the potential to feel and desire certain things, Satan has the ability to manipulate and misdirect those feelings and desires. That is the essence of temptation. Satan's appeal to you and me is to meet God-given needs and fulfill God-given desires the easiest, quickest, and least painful way."[34]

Instead of the appetite for food and water being disciplined for the good of the body, it can now be a means of experiencing pleasure or escaping emotional pressures and can become gluttony. Many illustrations of this corruption of the natural bodily appetites are found in the Bible. Eli, a good man and faithful priest of Israel, allowed his life and family to be destroyed as a result of a weak will that would not stand up to his sons' acts of disobedience and irreverence. This weakened will was developed over time through indulgence and gluttony in his appetite for food.[35] The prophet of Bethel, another outstanding servant of God, came to an untimely and unfortunate death because his appetite for food made him more susceptible to the deceit of an older prophet.[36]

The sexual appetite that was given for man's enjoyment and reproduction in marriage is now one of the greatest sources of temptation to sin. For this reason, instead of a married couple's joy being the only motivation needed for fulfilling this appetite, the Bible actually commands married couples to continually fulfill this appetite as a protection against the temptation of the

---

34   Stanley, *Winning the War Within*, 66
35   1 Samuel 2:29; 3:13; 4:17-18.
36   1 Kings 13:15-19.

Devil.[37] Much of the book of Proverbs deals with the dangers of temptation through the weakness of the flesh due to the corrupted natural appetites. Laziness is said to lead to poverty.[38] Lust and adultery are shown to have grave consequences.[39] James warns about temptation due to corruption in the flesh and how it seduces the will to sin, saying:

> *But every man is tempted, when he is drawn away of his own lust, and enticed. Then when lust hath conceived, it bringeth forth sin: and sin, when it is finished, bringeth forth death.* (James 1:14-15)

In many cases, this unrestrained and progressively degenerating course toward base sensuality becomes an expression of rebellion against God's order.

This corruption of the natural, God-given appetites gives way to the formation of unnatural "developed appetites." These include desires for such things as liquor, drugs, pornography, or music that satisfies the self-interest of the flesh. We must, therefore, distinguish between the corruption of the natural appetites and the formation of corrupt, unnatural appetites. Although they are related and similar, they are also different in that the corrupted, natural appetites are based upon natural, God-given, bodily needs, and the corrupted, unnatural, developed appetites are not based on natural bodily needs.

Eating and drinking in excess, without regard to nutrition, is an abuse of the body's natural need for food and drink. Alcoholism and drug abuse, although consumed by the body, are not related to natural appetites or needs of the body. Laziness is a type of gluttony in relation to the body's need for rest, and sensuality and immorality are abuses of the natural appetites for sexual relations. So-called homosexuality, on the other hand, is

---

37   1 Corinthians 7:5.

38   Proverbs 6:4-11.

39   Proverbs 2:16-18; 5:3-5; 6:27-29.

not based upon these natural appetites, but is rather developed by many other factors.

The developed appetites result in addictions and dependencies that are as strong as or stronger than the natural appetites. Whereas the correction of abuses of the natural appetites has to do with increasing understanding and discipline, the correction of developed appetites is generally more complicated. The question then is what are the factors in the formation of developed appetites? How do they come about in a person's life?

Simple curiosity comes to mind once again as a steppingstone to the development of unnatural appetites. Discovering how many people in history took the first step toward the formation of a habit of vice by simple curiosity would be amazing. This innate drive is the reason many take their first drink, smoke their first cigarette, try their first drug, or focus for the first time on a perverted sexual experience.

The desire for acceptance is another powerful drive that can result in developing unnatural appetites. The influence of a particular friend can be a strong driving force to initiate one or more of these practices. Peer pressure is another powerful force.

Stanley says, "As long as men and women seek to gain their sense of significance and self-worth from anything other than God, they will be set up for temptation. Certain people, places, or things will always have an inordinate ability to lure them into sin. Until they change their definition of significance and until they transfer their security to Someone who can give them real security, they will never experience lasting victory in their lives."[40]

Still another factor is the desire for escape. Hurtful circumstances or feelings may become such an overwhelming burden that escape is sought. The troubled person seeks relief by way of these developed appetites that seem to rescue the mind and emotions from facing depression or despair. Sometimes it is

---

40   Stanley, *Winning the War Within*, 50.

an escape from feelings such as inferiority and rejection; other times it is an escape from the hurt of tragedies, divorces, or similar losses.

Social customs in various cultures are another factor that is responsible for the development of unnatural appetites. In some cultures, being overweight is considered to be a sign of health and prosperity. Other customs include the use of alcohol and drugs in social or even religious practices. Still others promote sexual immorality in teenage boys as a part of their development of masculinity. A high degree of ignorance exists in these cases as to the harm done to the body and life.

Much more common is the factor of enticement. A tremendous amount of money is spent on these developed appetites, and many unscrupulous and greed-driven people use every means possible to entice unsuspecting people for profit. The natural weaknesses such as curiosity, desire for acceptance, desire for escape, or feelings of rebellion become tools for these people to provoke others to initiate and develop habits and addictions.

However, greed is not the only motivation for enticing others to fall into unnatural appetites. The desire for power and influence to promote wicked philosophies is another driving force behind those who lure others to their manner of living and thinking. Those who have given themselves over to evil and perverted lifestyles find great satisfaction in justifying their perversion by seducing others to follow them. These people are not content to find regular jobs to make a living. They want to be teachers, psychologists, lawmakers, news reporters, or anything they can be to spread the propaganda and the manipulative lies that may deceive others and entice them to the same wicked lifestyles. Promoters of homosexual perversion and nudism have become extremely adept at changing the language and meaning of words to justify wrong and condemn right. Now, those who *prohibit* their sodomy are considered "immoral."

Rebellion is also one of the most common causes of unnatural appetites. The practice of satisfying these appetites is their way of going against the order and authority of God and the type of society that he has established. As has been shown, rebellion can cause an experience with drugs and can become an emotional addiction that enslaves a person.

After considering these elements in the formation of developed, unnatural appetites, we can see the greater complexity of abusing the natural appetites. Understanding how these appetites have developed in one's own life or in the life of another will require much more from us. In addition, we need to know what steps are necessary to undo these dependencies that have added to the weakness of the flesh and have increased the susceptibility to temptation.

When God made man, he lovingly created his body with five senses capable of giving him great pleasure. Along with this capability, God created an environment where the experience of pleasure would become a daily reality. Sight was given not only for observation. God gave a sensation of pleasure when certain things are seen. To man these things became what is known as beauty. Not everything would give the same pleasure when seen. Otherwise, nothing would seem special, and the pleasure could not be appreciated. A meadow might be pleasant to see, but a crop of flowers would send special pleasure through this sense of sight.

The same holds true for each of the other senses: Smell, taste, hearing, and touch. Each sense would give man varying amounts of pleasure according to different circumstances and experiences, and man's joy would give constant testimony of God's goodness. The purity of this joy was another casualty of the fall, becoming corrupted just as in the case of the natural God-given appetites. As a result of this corruption, the same pleasure that was once for man's good can now result in his destruction. Because of this, pleasure can now be very deceitful.

Screwtape reveals the Devil's work in this area, saying: "I know we have won many a soul through pleasure. All the same, it is His invention, not ours. He made the pleasures: All our research so far has not enabled us to produce one. All we can do is to encourage the humans to take the pleasures which our Enemy has produced, at times, or in ways, or in degrees, which He has forbidden."[41]

Because pleasure brings joy, the natural desire is to repeat that which produced the sensation. However, a great number of pleasurable things end up causing great pain and damage either to oneself or to others.

God gave man a special experience of pleasure when he looks upon the body of his wife. Fallen man, however, finds that this pleasure is experienced by looking upon the bodies of other women also. The pleasure is real and enjoyable, but it is also deceitful because of the consequences that follow. The wisdom and blessings of God that are essential to one's true well-being are sacrificed. Self-control and personal discipline are weakened, and man becomes susceptible to losing control, causing him possible damage. Shame and fear can result in dishonesty that will undermine the trust in relations necessary for true satisfaction. Broken relationships and marriages are often the result of giving in to the desire for pleasure out of the order that God established. Pleasure produces joy, but the joy soon passes, and the pain and heartache remain.

Each sense can be deceitful. Smell is used to allure one to sensuality. Taste can be pleasurable and yet result in bodily damage, pain, and even death. Touch can be especially deceitful and tempt one in all forms of sensuality. Consider this truth in relation to the sense of hearing. Today's controversy over contemporary

---

41   Lewis, *Screwtape Letters*, 49.

Christian music must take into consideration this concept. Not only is the popular volume deceitful in that it is harmful to the bodily organ created for hearing, styles of music also bring consequences. Much of today's popular music has created stubborn, defensive attitudes in both young people and adults to the point that there is a willingness to sacrifice relationships with parents, relatives, friends, and churches. Standards and modesty are weakened, leaving people susceptible to still other forms of temptation. The unselfish quality of thinking first of others, *lest I make my brother to offend*,[42] is sacrificed, resulting in little concern about being a negative influence or *stumbling block* to others.[43] Future generations grow up with a concept of "my way" Christianity, sacrificing the attitude of self-denial and submission to Christ that is necessary to make the proper, wise choices in life's greatest decisions. These wrong decisions bring lasting pain and harm.

This analysis of the weakness of the flesh paints a very bleak picture. The degree of weakness is greater than is normally understood and could cause one to lose hope of ever overcoming temptation. The opposite is actually true. When one comes to understand how utterly weak the flesh is, he can stop depending on any personal, natural strength. In so doing, he opens the door to learning and experiencing the power that overcomes temptation.

---

42   1 Corinthians 8:13.
43   Romans 14:13.

The Attraction of the World

U nfortunately, we must continue to expand this bleak picture of the weakness of the flesh, adding to it the power of the influences and attraction of the world. By "world" we refer to the systems, order, and philosophies of life that are not what God planned and ordained for mankind. The non-biblical world system is a result of the weakness of the flesh and the deceit of Satan. This system plays upon the weakness of the flesh which leaves man vulnerable to ever greater conformity to the world. Distinguishing between what proceeds from the weakness of the flesh and what comes from the attraction of the world is difficult. Sensuality is certainly due to the weakness of the flesh, but it is also identified as an attraction of the world. Appetites are a factor in the weakness of the flesh, and yet the world capitalizes on this weakness for commercial gain.

Riches

Some areas are especially associated with the attraction of the world. The first of these is what Jesus called *the deceit of riches* in the parable of the sower in Matthew 13:22. Throughout history, we find man's acute susceptibility to riches. Balaam was a prophet of God who received special revelation. Even so, he was overcome by the deceit of riches and died as one of the particularly wicked men in the Bible.[44] Achan knew very well of the curse put upon the spoil of Jericho, but he could not resist

---

44   Numbers 22; Jude 11.

taking gold and garments. He also died in infamy.[45] The rich young ruler[46] personally met Jesus. He knew he was from God and had seen miracles and works that testified of this truth. He was given the rare chance to become a disciple who followed and lived with Christ. Yet, this power also overcame him and he gave up the opportunity, choosing his worldly riches instead.

There are a great number of Scriptures in the Bible dealing with the danger of being allured by the deceit of riches. Consider a few examples:

> *The graven images of their gods shall ye burn with fire: thou shalt not desire the silver or gold that is on them, nor take it unto thee, lest thou be snared therein: for it is an abomination to the LORD thy God.* (Deut. 7:25)

> *My son, if sinners entice thee, consent thou not. If they say, Come with us, let us lay wait for blood, let us lurk privily for the innocent without cause: Let us swallow them up alive as the grave; and whole, as those that go down into the pit: We shall find all precious substance, we shall fill our houses with spoil: Cast in thy lot among us; let us all have one purse: My son, walk not thou in the way with them; refrain thy foot from their path: For their feet run to evil, and make haste to shed blood.* (Proverbs 1:10-16)

> *But they that will be rich fall into temptation and a snare, and into many foolish and hurtful lusts, which drown men in destruction and perdition. For the love of money is the root of all evil: which while some coveted after, they have erred from the faith, and pierced themselves through with many sorrows.* (1 Timothy 6:9-10)

45   Joshua 7:21.
46   Mark 10:21.

Why is it that so many people fall into this snare? How is it that the desire for riches can trap a person to the point that he will sacrifice family, the blessing of God, reputation, or almost anything if he supposes that the end result will be the gain of riches? This temptation has always abounded. War and death has often been the end result of greed. Today the world plays upon this desire. One greedy man or group entices others with the same greed, knowing how effective it will be. Gambling, lotteries, pyramid schemes, and "get-rich-quick" investment schemes give evidence of the power that the deceit of riches has over man. Most people have fond imaginations of what it would be like to be wealthy, and if some "lucky" opportunity comes up that appears to be a way of making that imagination a reality, it becomes a tremendous temptation.

Of course, we know from the examples of Abraham and Job in the Bible that there is nothing wrong with being wealthy. Even God uses wealth as a blessing and reward, as in the case of Solomon. Why then are riches so effective a snare? The answer to this question again goes back to the consequences of the fall of man. Adam and Eve had every need provided for and were void of any sense of lack or insecurity. Fallen man lives under the curse of having to provide his needs by the sweat of his brow.[47] He faces the possibility of drought, famine, floods, fires, or other natural disaster that are out of his control but result in either a fear of lack or the actual experience of lack.

What, he asks, could give him the security he needs in order to have no fear? To this question the world answers, wealth. If you have enough money, you will have no fear. It seems clear and logical, and therein we find the elements of the deceit of riches. Jesus opened our eyes to the fallacy of this logic when he said, *lay not up for yourselves treasures upon earth where moth and rust doth corrupt and where thieves break through*

---

47   Genesis 3:19.

and steal.[48] Far from producing peace and security, riches only increase the possibility of loss with its tormenting sense of insecurity. There are multitudes of causes for the loss of wealth. Some are natural as symbolized by *moth and rust.* Others are results of the depravity of man as symbolized in *thieves break through and steal.*

This last reason for loss brings us to another element involved in the deceit of riches. Not only does man now have an inherent fear of lack due to the insecurity of a cursed world, he also has the depraved, selfish heart that cares about his own well-being to the point of putting his own needs and desires first, even if this causes harm to others.

Man has devised every way possible to take money and goods away from others in order to add to his own wealth. Direct thievery is always rampant and becoming more and more sophisticated with time. However, man has developed many ways of plundering others besides break-ins. Investment scams are abundant and merchandise scams are no less. Even taxes levied by governments are used for personal political gain or skimmed off through devious accounting procedures. These thieves, however, live under the same threat from others, so they may never achieve the purposes that wealth seems to offer.

This brings us to the third element in the deceit of riches. Earlier I mentioned how a baby will learn that by crying it can have its needs satisfied. Later, however, the baby becomes aware that even when it does not need anything, crying can achieve selfish desires. This principle is also part of the deceit of riches. We find that riches do not satisfy. Even when a person has wealth, he feels the need to obtain more. There is a story about a person asking a rich man how much wealth he needed. The rich man answered, "Just a little more." The satisfaction and security that riches seem to offer is never achieved. It is

---

48   Matthew 6:19.

deceitful, however, in that wealth appears to offer security and satisfaction. As a result, we live in a world where riches are sought by both poor and rich alike (even if it causes harm, loss, or destruction of others), but in the end, the riches fail to give what they appeared to offer.

Solomon wrote of this deceit in the book of Ecclesiastes. A study of chapter 2 reveals how he sought to find fulfillment in life. He was rich and nothing was beyond his reach. He used his riches to provide laughter, music, servants, houses, vineyards, gardens, orchards, silver, gold, and the most exotic treasures. He could say that *whatsoever mine eyes desired, I kept not from them.*[49] Far from the satisfaction he sought, however, he gave testimony that the end result was only *vanity and vexation of spirit*[50] or, in other words, emptiness and sorrow.

The final element in the deceit of riches is found in the cases where the accumulation of wealth has achieved its purpose. With great distress, Asaph lamented, *I was envious at the foolish, when I saw the prosperity of the wicked.*[51] Job also referred to the fact that at times the wicked prosper, saying: *The tabernacles of robbers prosper, and they that provoke God are secure; into whose hand God bringeth abundantly.*[52] They not only become wealthy and powerful, they oppress others and even deny God. Yet, they seem to be above the consequences and worries that others experience. They have achieved all that man could want, and it appears that, in their case, riches were not deceitful after all. Temptation for them "paid off."

Job used this fact to counter the assumption made by his friends that all sinners suffer and that suffering was an evidence of sin. Asaph was distressed by the prosperity of the wicked, because he was suffering in spite of his faithfulness to God.

49   Ecclesiastes 2:10.
50   Ecclesiastes 2:11.
51   Psalm 73:3.
52   Job 12:6.

The injustice turned out to be deceit after all when Asaph saw the larger picture of reality. He understood that if riches and power were all a man had in this life, it was of no more value than a dream, because this life will end. Besides finding that all material things would be lost, he would face eternal damnation. That was not something to envy after all.

In spite of the knowledge Christ gave to shed light on the reality of the deceit of riches, man continues to assume that wealth is the solution. The world continues to appear attractive.

Power and Popularity

Apart from the world's influence through sensual seduction and the deceit of riches, the world also tempts in the area of pride. *The pride of life*, as John calls it,[53] shows up in many different ways. The two most common are power and popularity. Both are intermingled with the deceit of riches, and it is sometimes difficult to separate them. However, power and popularity involve other circumstances besides wealth.

When I use the term power, I refer to the ability of a person to impose his will on others. Power includes strength, force, and control. Sometimes this power is a part of wealth, but often it is a part of the person's social standing or position. Man's inherent pride makes him desire to be above others, not below. This varies according to a man's temperament, circumstances, and experience. The choleric temperament has a natural tendency to strive for positions of power because of his drive to accomplish projects. The phlegmatic has less drive for positions of power. Circumstances that add to this natural desire of pride may be related to social standing or family. Children or friends of powerful people often believe they inherently have the same power.

The experience of oppression can drive men to a point where their only desire in life is to get out from under another's power

---

53   1 John 2:16.

and take the power themselves, as can be witnessed in street gangs. Other times it has to do with having had a taste of power and becoming addicted to its sensation. Wise Solomon warned against the possibility of being seduced by this thirst for power, saying: *The righteous is more excellent than his neighbour: but the way of the wicked seduceth them.*[54] Whatever the case, man has a natural desire to be first and to control others.

Therefore, when the world offers a way to fulfill this desire for power, a great temptation arises to sacrifice relationships, integrity, and even family. Tragedy occurred when Solomon's own son, Rehoboam, disregarded the admonitions of his father and the advice of his father's wise counselors, when his peers filled his head with thoughts of power and greatness above what his father had experienced. The end result was the division of the kingdom, a great loss of power, and the shame of having acted foolishly.[55]

Similar to this attraction of riches is the attraction of popularity. Popularity is based upon what the particular group in a society values. Although values vary from culture to culture, most often they are based upon a person's appearance, intelligence, or talents. Appearance includes a person's beauty, color, and stature but also depends upon styles and fads. People's desire for acceptance and popularity drives them to seek an appearance that others will value. The world is able to capitalize on this desire. Offers of exercise machines or routines, diets and other weight control schemes are endless. Billions of dollars are spent on makeup, skin treatments, clothing, jewelry, and popular music. People think that if they can have the right styles, color of hair, or tennis shoes, they will feel good about themselves and be accepted or even popular. Knowing this, the world continually tries to redefine what that "right look" includes.

54   Proverbs 12:26.
55   1 Kings 12.

Of course, the world's corruption goes further than just commercializing the desire for acceptance and popularity. The world also desires to establish its own standards of right and wrong and thereby eliminate responsibility to God.

After appearance, the world values intelligence. No one wants to appear "dumb," so the world offers many ways and means to appear otherwise. Besides the legitimate efforts through private education, tutoring, and extracurricular studies, cheating is also considered acceptable if needed. The appearance of intelligence is so much more valuable to the world than honesty and integrity that it is difficult to find those who would not cheat even if they could do well honestly. The appearance of intelligence is also commercialized, because it is the actual, underlying reason for having many of the possessions that have to do with information, such as computer accessories, cell phones, and other technological tools. It is not enough to have a tool that works. It has to be popular.

Third in the order of values for popularity is talent or other outstanding capability. Sports and music skills are some of the most valued talents, along with acting and art. Again, great emphasis is placed upon being popular through talents, and the world astutely commercializes this as well.

Of course, good appearance, intellect, or talent is not wrong. The temptation that the world offers has to do with valuing these things over the qualities that God esteems the highest in value. Popularity in the world includes sacrificing God's values of honesty, moral purity, unselfishness, and so forth. In the world's system, if lying is necessary to achieve or protect popularity, then telling the truth is a hindrance, a weakness, and unwise. Much popularity is gained at the expense of other competitors, and unselfishness would be considered foolish. In the same way, moral purity is considered prudish and mocked because it is not popular. Herein lies the deceit of the temptation of the *pride of life.*

Sadly, for all the rush and struggle to conform to the world's values in appearance, intellect, or talent, the individual comes up short. A person's appearance normally does not fit the mold. Something is always not quite right. Or, even if a few people do seem to be everything the world values in these ways, they find that power and popularity are empty and void of the satisfaction they desire. Worse yet, they find that they have destroyed the true elements that are necessary to find that satisfaction by having cast away God's values in their quest for the world's values. A happy, united marriage and family, genuine friends, an honorable reputation, and a clear conscience are seen as some of the true treasures of life but may now be impossible or improbable goals as a consequence of having lived according to a lifestyle that the world deceived the individual into seeking.

CHAPTER 5

The Fiery Darts of Satan

O ur struggle with the overwhelming weakness of the flesh and the deceitful attraction of the world is bad enough, but the situation is much worse. Man also has an intelligent and deviously wicked enemy. This enemy is most often called Satan or the Devil. He is referred to as the prince of the power of the air, the god of this world, the deceiver, the father of lies, the accuser of the brethren, and other terms that describe his wickedness, his purposes, and the continual battle he wages against mankind. The intelligence of Satan is difficult to comprehend, as he was created for special service before God. He is now void of anything that is good and is, on the contrary, the essence of evil. He understands how to use the weakness of a man's flesh against him and how to increase that weakness. The world system is in his power, and he delights in creating an ever-expanding corruption of all values and good created by God.

It was by his subtle temptation that man fell and sin entered into the world, and he now wreaks havoc through his work of tempting fallen man. His attacks are symbolically called *fiery darts*,[56] which implies the damage and destruction that he can bring to lives, families, nations, and even to the works of the church. Great power is in his hands. He has an army of spiritual underlings called demons who, under certain conditions, can possess the bodies and minds of men such that they may suffer painful torments, harm themselves, and even exercise

---

56   Ephesians 6:16.

supernatural strength. Besides this, Satan has the capability to perform great *signs and wonders*[57] to create fear and deception.

His Use of Ignorance

However, even with his great power, few of Satan's wicked works involve using this power. He knows that he can do much more damage in another way. For the most part, he does not use signs and wonders, because his greatest asset is the fact that most people do not even think about him. This common ignorance of his work is the perfect smokescreen that enables him to continue doing his evil works unnoticed until his purposes are fulfilled.

This is what C. S. Lewis's demon, Screwtape, meant when he told his demon nephew, "I wonder you should ask me whether it is essential to keep the patient in ignorance of your own existence. That question, at least for the present phase of the struggle, has been answered for us by the High Command. Our policy, for the moment, is to conceal ourselves."[58]

If people were to see too much evidence of his presence, it would defeat this primary opportunity to work unnoticed and, therefore, unhindered. In spite of his supernatural abilities, he is very limited. All power in heaven and on earth belongs to Christ, and Satan can do nothing that God does not allow. Through the work of Christ upon the cross, the power of Satan was defeated, and God has given his children power to resist and defeat Satan. Even those who are not the children of God have enough freedom of will to oppose Satan's work in their lives and turn to God.

For this reason, Satan does his work in the "darkness," while remaining unknown, fully aware that if he can do his work this way, he will be unhindered. Few people, even Christians,

---

57   Mark 13:22.
58   Lewis, *Screwtape Letters,* 39.

are aware of the presence and subtle work of the Devil in their day-to-day living. Satan has achieved much when people do not learn of his tactics, and they even feel embarrassed to talk about him. He is known to exist along with his evil cohorts, but such knowledge is vague and theoretical, not objective and practical. Our lack of awareness increases our susceptibility to temptation.

It is quite astounding to discover that for all his intelligence, Satan is not exceptionally original in his work. The methods he used throughout history as described in the Bible are the same methods he uses against man today. Therefore, we can understand his tactics, and through this understanding, learn to defeat him. Paul said, *we are not ignorant of his devices.*[59] With this in mind, let us analyze what tactics Satan used in the past and apply this knowledge to what we observe today.

His Goal

When we go back to the beginning of Satan's evil, we find that his fall was due to vanity or pride in desiring to have his own way apart from the will of God. His desire to be like God was evil in that it was directly against the will of God. This is the essence of sin and evil: To exercise one's will in one's own way, not in submission to God's will. Isaiah described the essence or base of all sin, saying: *all we like sheep have gone astray. We have turned every one to his own way.*[60] In consequence to this sin of pride or willfulness, Satan lost his glory, was cast down, and was condemned to an eternity in the place of torment prepared for him, the lake of fire. Through this experience, he knows that if man will also exercise his own will instead of the will of God, evil and destruction follow. This goal would fulfill any evil desire for vengeance against God. He could feel

---

59   2 Corinthians 2:11.

60   Isaiah 53:6.

a wicked pleasure in taking away from God's glory and ruining the communion God desires to have with man.

Stanley says, "Simply put, the point is that *you do not struggle with temptation in a vacuum.* Every temptation you encounter is Satan's way of striking out against God. By attempting to introduce into your life disorder and chaos, Satan continues his work of undoing all God sought to accomplish in the beginning. On the other hand, every victory you experience is a testimony to both Satan and the world that God is at work restoring things to their original state, a state in which Satan has no place or power."[61]

Considering the weakness of the flesh and the attraction of the world, this goal of getting man to think and act according to his own will does not seem difficult. The apostle Paul understood this susceptibility of man to the deceitful devices of the Devil. He wrote to his beloved churches in Corinth with fear that they were falling prey to Satan's lies and to the lies of those false teachers that he already controlled, saying:

> *But I fear, lest by any means, as the serpent beguiled Eve through his subtilty, so your minds should be corrupted from the simplicity that is in Christ . . . And no marvel; for Satan himself is transformed into an angel of light. Therefore it is no great thing if his ministers also be transformed as the ministers of righteousness; whose end shall be according to their works.* (2 Corinthians 11:3, 14-15)

The Subconscious Mind
One of the reasons the Devil is so effective in causing man to act according to his own will is the way man's mind works. The mind has both conscious activity and subconscious activity.

---

61 Stanley, *Winning the War Within*, 31.

During the mind's conscious activity, man is fully aware of his thoughts, actions, time, and purposes. Satan can attempt to deceive man even when he is conscious, as we will see. However, his greatest access to man's mind is during subconscious activity. The article on the word *subconscious* in the *World Book Encyclopedia* begins with the explanation that "Subconscious is a term to describe mental processes such as thoughts, ideas and feelings that go on in people's minds without their being aware of them."[62] The lack of awareness during this type of mental activity is a perfectly effective smokescreen for Satan to sow thoughts that lead the mind to dwell on sin. This is so well known that one of our most common "wise sayings" is "an idle mind is the Devil's workshop."

That Satan has this direct access to man's mind is apparent from Scripture. After Jesus told the parable of the sower, he later explained that *When any one heareth the word of the kingdom, and understandeth it not, then cometh the wicked one, and catcheth away that which was sown in his heart.*[63] By this we realize Satan somehow knows if there is or is not understanding in the mind of man. Not only does he have this knowledge, he has access to the mind and the ability to take something away from the mind. The fact that he can put thoughts into the mind is demonstrated in the incident of Ananias and Sapphira. They had conspired to lie about the amount of money that had been received from the sale of property and brought as an offering to the Lord. Peter revealed, however, that Satan had placed that thought in their minds, saying: *Ananias, why hath Satan filled thine heart to lie to the Holy Ghost, and to keep back part of the price of the land?*[64]

Paul also declared how Satan was able to blind the minds

---

62   "Subconscious," *The World Book Encyclopedia*, 1979 ed.

63   Matthew 13:19.

64   Acts 5:3.

of the people who do not believe.[65] This also appears to be a direct manipulation of thoughts. In addition, he alludes to this capability of Satan when he speaks of *bringing into captivity every thought to the obedience of Christ.*[66]

C. S. Lovett says, "Clearly the center of our warfare is our mind. If Satan can keep Christians from storing God's Word, their prime weapon against him is gone. If he can cause a mind to flit among the trash and trivia of our day, it will be useless to the Holy Spirit. Since he has the power to introduce ideas, mental wondering is accomplished easily. The mind, also the channel for the Spirit of God, is quickly blocked with foolish imaginations and notions."[67]

Some of the thoughts that Satan uses to steer subconscious thinking come from man's own memory. This is one of the reasons, perhaps, that Paul warned the Romans to be *wise unto that which is good, and simple concerning evil.*[68] The more our minds are exposed to ungodly thoughts, words, or sights, the more material Satan has to work with from within our own memories. Other thoughts are fabricated by the mind's ability to form imaginations. These imaginations may take material from the memory, or they may be entirely made up. In most cases, the subconscious probably uses a combination of both memory and imagination.

Whatever the case, we need to understand how Satan uses this subconscious "day dreaming" as an open opportunity to tempt the mind to focus on sinful thoughts and imaginations. It is a common experience for someone to be shocked when all of a sudden their mind returns to conscious thinking, and they become aware of the wickedness that is going on in their mind. Sometimes there is no memory of how that thought originated,

---

65 2 Corinthians 4:4.

66 2 Corinthians 10:5.

67 C. S. Lovett, *Dealing With the Devil* (Baldwin Park: Personal Christianity, 1967), 37.

68 Romans 16:19.

which is what Satan would most likely desire. However, the mind is capable of recalling the chain of thoughts that one experienced. To our surprise, Satan can use an innocent thought or memory to cause the mind to go into its subconscious state and use that thought to trigger another memory or idea. Gradually, he can lead the mind, thought by thought, to the wicked imagination that becomes the focus of the mind.

Because this subconscious state of the mind is such an easy opportunity for Satan to tempt the mind to sin, we must recognize the extreme importance of avoiding experiences in which the mind will obtain sights, words, and ideas that will fill the memory with tools for Satan's attacks. Undoubtedly, television programs or even commercials are the prime source of Satan's tools in this day and age. Parents should be very aware of the damage television can do to their children and of the struggles their children will have as a consequence. One of the most stupid, but effective, lies of the Devil is the concept that indecent, evil programs are "for adults only." If anything, adults' minds are even more susceptible to this evil, because their understanding is so much greater than that of young children. Anyone and everyone will suffer consequences if their minds are filled with indecent, wicked thoughts and ideas.

Other sources of evil thoughts that Satan can use in the subconscious are literature, radio, music, and people who freely express evil thoughts and feelings. One of the fundamental reasons for modern Christian education is to protect children from corrupting ideas that come from friends or even teachers in secular education. Responsible, loving parents must do everything possible to avoid experiences that corrupt their own minds and the minds of their children.

On this danger, Owen warns, "It is sad to find most people so careless about this. Most people think about how to avoid open sin, but they never think about the dynamics of temptation within their hearts. How readily young people mix with all sorts of company. Before they realize it, they enjoy evil company. Then it is too late to warn them about the dangers of wrong companions. Unless God snatches them in a mighty way from the jaws of destruction, they will be lost."[69]

However, avoiding these experiences in this world is not possible, and in many cases avoiding people whose communication is full of corrupting thoughts is not even right. We are responsible to be an active, positive influence in the lives of some of these people. Jesus said that we must be *the light of the world* and *the salt of the earth*[70] which implies direct, continual association with these people. When Paul rebuked the Corinthians for their wrong attitude in continuing to associate themselves with an adulterous man, he said, *I have written unto you not to keep company, if any man that is called a brother be a fornicator, or covetous, or an idolater, or a railer, or a drunkard, or an extortioner; with such an one no not to eat.* However, he explained that he was not talking about avoiding people in the world who lived in these sins: *Yet not altogether with the fornicators of this world, or with the covetous, or extortioners, or with idolaters; for then must ye needs go out of the world.*[71] Jesus himself expressed the correct attitude toward this problem of association with the people of this world when he prayed for his disciples, saying: *I pray not that thou shouldest take them out of the world but that thou shouldest keep them from the evil.*[72] Someone wisely said "a boat must be in the water, but the water must not be in the boat." We cannot and in many cases should not avoid association with people of the world in spite of the exposure to corruption through their words and actions.

---

69   Owen, *Sin and Temptation,* 122.
70   Matthew 5:13.
71   1 Corinthians 5:9-11.
72   John 17:15.

However, we must not allow them to be an evil influence over us, but rather; we must be a positive, spiritual influence over them.

Even this course of action has its limitations, as we are told by Jesus not to *cast our pearls before swine*.[73] Many shameful situations must be avoided. While children are still maturing, they must be protected from situations, friends, and teachers whose influence could overcome them or give Satan an opportunity to tempt and deceive them. However, since God expects us to be a direct, positive influence in the lives of ungodly people in this world, avoiding exposure to corruption is not the only answer. God has also made the mind capable of self-discipline in order to reject the thoughts that Satan could later use to tempt us. Not only has he given the mind this capability, he has also made us responsible to exercise it.

As mentioned before, the will of man is the prize that Satan seeks. He desires to influence the will and to provoke man to act according to his own will instead of submitting himself to God. His work in the subconscious activity of the mind is not just to cause evil imaginations and torment; his goal is to cause the mind to influence the will.

Owen explains, "The mind is the leading faculty of the soul. When the mind fixes upon an object or course of action, the will and the affections follow suit. They are incapable of any other consideration. Thus, while the entanglement of the affections in sin is often very troublesome, it is the deceit of the mind that is always the most dangerous situation because of its role in all other operations of the soul."[74]

This is accomplished by the formation of conclusions in the mind. Mere thoughts and imaginations are easily accepted or rejected by the mind. However, once the mind forms conclusions, the will is dominated by them. Conclusions, as Satan well

---

73   Matthew 7:6.
74   Owen, *Sin and Temptation*, 36-37.

knows, have little to do with truth. False conclusions dominate the will as well as those based on truth. Sincerity is also no problem for Satan. Being sincerely wrong is as easy as being sincerely right. Conclusions do not even have to be logical to dominate the will.

The battle then is to form conclusions in the mind. God gives man his Word of truth and a capability to reject error. With these tools, man is capable of forming right conclusions and enjoying the security and joy that results. Satan uses his subtlety and deceit to cause man to reject or distort the truth, so man will form false conclusions and act according to them.

Owen's insight is helpful as he states, "We also see the danger of sin's deception of the mind by examining the general nature of deceit. It consists in falsely presenting things to the mind in such a way that their true nature, causes, effects, or present conditions to the soul remain hidden. Thus deceit conceals what should be exposed, whether it be circumstances or consequences.

"Just as Satan deceived our first parents, he continues to do so today by misrepresentation. The fruit was desirable; that was obvious to the eye. Satan then secretly suggested that God sought to limit their happiness by forbidding them to eat it. But Satan hid from them the fact that this was a test of their obedience, and that certain if not immediate ruin would ensue if they disobeyed God. Satan deceived them by simply proposing immediate gratification, which the fruit certainly provided. This is the nature of deceit. By only presenting the desirable aspects of temptation, it deceives the mind into making a false judgment."[75]

However, the easy access to the subconscious activity of the mind and the work he does there is actually only a means to an end, because for the most part the will is controlled by conscious

---

75   Owen, *Sin and Temptation*, 37.

activity of the mind. Satan desires to see man choose his own will and disregard God's will in a fully conscious manner.

The Conscious Mind

The *fiery darts*, or tools, that Satan uses to tempt us were demonstrated from the beginning in the garden of Eden. All of these tools involve deceit, since he has to convince man to disregard the perfect, wise, and eternal will of God and follow his own imperfect, ignorant ways. Satan's first tactic then was to present himself in the form of something outwardly beautiful. Eve would accept this as she was given the ability to appreciate beauty and, without thinking, could feel that anything so pleasing as beauty must be good. The deceit began in this way due to her not knowing that outward beauty is not necessarily related to good.

Satan is an expert in using appearances that are acceptable and pleasing in order to catch man off guard. Still today many forms of vice and sin are painted as being a part of something beautiful. The "Marlboro Man" was handsome and ruggedly attractive. He rode a beautiful horse in some breathtaking countryside. Many cigarettes were sold on his message, but in the end as he was dying of cancer, the truth was known. Instead of being the way to the good life, the beautiful message led to death. Liquor, gambling, and immorality are whitewashed in the same way – using beauty to lead man to see it as something good. Drugs are being related to health and painkilling, and tolerance of sexual perversion is painted as compassionate, fair, and socially mature. Nothing is painted as attractive, however, as "doing your own thing" and enjoying yourself, the very way that sin came into existence.

Along with this appearance of beauty, Satan gave the impression that he was interested in Eve's well-being and sorry if she was deprived of anything. The subtle devious comment that he put into a question, *hath God said, ye shall not eat of every tree of the garden?*[76] softly implied that she was being deprived and he was concerned for her. The question would make her think of an answer but with a distorted version of God's command. Out of his of mercy and goodness, God had instructed them to eat of all the trees in the garden that he had created for their delight and well-being. There were miles and miles of good things to enjoy and just one single tree that they were to abstain from because of the harm it would bring. All of this was painted differently by Satan's question. He turned the whole focus of God's command toward the prohibited tree, questioning the reason for such a "strict" prohibition and insinuating that Eve was being deprived instead of cared for.

Satan continues using this tactic today, and it is still effective in accomplishing his deceitful purpose. He distorts the meaning and purpose of circumstances in a way that will get man's mind off the principles of right and wrong, or good and evil, and will instead focus it on whether it seems "fair or just." Politicians have become the exceptional students of this tactic and approach the ability of Satan himself in their ability to insinuate that people are deprived victims due to the unfair ways of others. The whole liberal political movement depends upon this tactic of the Devil and could not survive without it. The seeming concern for others is as fraudulent as was Satan's supposed concern for the well-being of Eve. In truth, those who use this tactic only desire to use people for their own ends, as Satan did Eve.

Having developed his plan of deceit by fraudulently gaining credibility through the appearance of beauty, an alleged interest in her well-being, and an apparent concern that she was being deprived, Satan took the final step in this temptation. He had gotten her mind off God and his will and, indirectly, caused

---

76   Genesis 3:1.

her to doubt his goodness and purposes. Still, there remained the fear of the Lord and of the consequence of disobedience, which would prevent her from eating the forbidden fruit. Satan's final subtle attack was on this fear of the Lord. He attempted to take away this fear by making an authoritative declaration, *Ye shall not surely die.*[77]

He set himself up as an expert who could explain to her the "real truth." Rather than die, she would be wise like God, which is something to be desired. He further declared that God knew this to be true. He stopped here and allowed her to use the insinuation to form a conclusion about God's goodness and motives. She may not have consciously thought such a thing, but the doubt had been sown. The lust of her flesh had been excited by the imagined good taste of the fruit. The lust of her eyes had been excited by the good appearance of the fruit. Finally, Satan achieved the excitement of the pride of life by seducing her with the thought of being like God in wisdom.

There was beauty. There was goodness. There was concern. There was a new understanding of the truth, and fear had been alleviated. Only good and satisfaction would result, so she took the fruit and ate it. Satan had no power over her. He had nothing of true goodness to offer. His way led to death. Yet, he was successful.

Was it easy to seduce Eve? She had no knowledge of evil and its threat. She had no experience or examples to learn from. Or is it easier to seduce the Christian today? He has plenty of knowledge of evil, experience, and examples to learn from, but he has the fallen flesh to contend with. Whatever the case, Satan is successful in using temptation to bring about sin. The story that God recorded in his Word about Satan and Eve reveals to us much of the tactics and mind of Satan. He will try to gain credibility through something that seems good. Paul said he

---

77   Genesis 3:4.

appears as an *angel of light*.[78] He subtly casts doubt on God's purposes and goodness. He provides authoritative, "expert" information that alleviates the fear of the Lord and the consequences of disobedience. All the while, he plans, organizes, and manipulates circumstances to appeal to the lust of the flesh, the lust of the eyes, and the pride of life. This is his two-sided attack. The world is used to appeal to the flesh outwardly, and inwardly the mind is swayed.

False Teachers

Satan knows that if he can capture the mind of a man, he is not far from capturing his will.[79] There are many ways to sow thoughts in the mind. In Eve's case, it was through conversation. Satan has many false teachers sowing lies and misinformation in others' minds. Some of these false teachers are deceived themselves, and others knowingly deceive for various evil reasons. Radio, television, and movies make it possible to sow this deceit in the minds of multitudes at the same time.

Similar to speech communication is the use of the written word. Satan effectively uses newspapers, magazines, books, and other forms of the printed word to sow deceit in the minds of the readers. In all of these outward ways, Satan uses the same tactics. He tries to create credibility in some way. This credibility is not based on principles of truth and the difference between right and wrong as established by God. Instead, his credibility developed through something superficial like the beauty of the serpent in Eve's case. Sometimes popularity and peer pressure create credibility. In other cases, it is based upon supposed expert training and educational degrees. It may be fame or political clout. Financial power is another base for supposed credibility.

---

78   2 Corinthians 11:14.
79   Proverbs 23:7 "For as he thinketh in his heart, so is he."

Along with some basis or claim to credibility, the deceiver portrays a mask of concern for the well-being of others. This concern may include financial deprivation, emotional abuse, environmental damage, future security, handicaps, spiritual needs, and an endless list of other supposed concerns. The vague, undefined concept of human rights is being effectively used to replace God's standards and laws of good and evil. Proven criminals and even murderers are set free in the name of defending human rights.

Credibility and concern, however, are only steps of preparation. The culmination of deceit and temptation is the use of authoritative, "expert" declarations that serve to usurp the authority and will of God himself. Some people have a natural inclination to accept something that appears to be said with authority. Authority seems to lend a sense of security, which is a strong need with many people. Others are inclined to believe these declarations simply because they want to. They may excuse wrong in their lifestyles or it may be the pride of wanting to be right about something. Whatever the case, Satan knows that with the proper preparation, an authoritative declaration will be as effective today as it was in Eden.

Knowledge of Specific Weaknesses

Satan's success in temptation through deceit is not only due to this subtle process of gaining credibility, but also to the apparently expert knowledge he has of man's tendencies and weaknesses. Each individual always seems to have a special "stumbling block" that has the potential to make him act according to his own will. God is also aware of these tendencies and sometimes allows Satan to tempt man in order to build his faith, loyalty, humility, and character. The clearest example of God allowing Satan to test man's strength of character is seen in the story of Job. In this case, God received glory when, after all of

Satan's work in destroying Job's material possessions, family, and health, he demonstrated a loyalty to God that demolished Satan's reasoning and accusations. God also used the trial to prove Job and teach him a depth of humility that even he had not experienced.

Some of the greatest men of character have fallen before a particular "stumbling block" used by Satan. God allowed one of the most faithful kings of Judah, Hezekiah, to be tested by Satan's devices. When Hezekiah was faced by overwhelming threats and enemies, he remained strong and experienced great victories.[80] Satan then used the flattery of apparent admirers. The Babylonians traveled far to show respect to him when he had been sick and to *enquire of the wonder that was done in the land.*[81] Isaiah records this failure saying:

> *At that time Merodachbaladan, the son of Baladan, king of Babylon, sent letters and a present to Hezekiah: for he had heard that he had been sick, and was recovered. And Hezekiah was glad of them, and shewed them the house of his precious things, the silver, and the gold, and the spices, and the precious ointment, and all the house of his armour, and all that was found in his treasures: there was nothing in his house, nor in all his dominion, that Hezekiah shewed them not. Then came Isaiah the prophet unto king Hezekiah, and said unto him, What said these men? and from whence came they unto thee? And Hezekiah said, They are come from a far country unto me, even from Babylon. Then said he, What have they seen in thine house? And Hezekiah answered, All that is in mine house have they seen: there is nothing*

---

80   2 Kings 18-19.
81   2 Chronicles 32:31.

among my treasures that I have not shewed them.
Then said Isaiah to Hezekiah, Hear the word of the
LORD of hosts: Behold, the days come, that all that
is in thine house, and that which thy fathers have
laid up in store until this day, shall be carried to
Babylon: nothing shall be left, saith the LORD. And
of thy sons that shall issue from thee, which thou
shalt beget, shall they take away; and they shall be
eunuchs in the palace of the king of Babylon.[82]

Hezekiah was blind in the face of this new temptation. His defenses were completely down, and he allowed vanity to overcome him and cause him to act according to his own will.

A similar example is the story of Gideon. He faced an overwhelming enemy and did not consider himself adequate to face them.[83] Besides this, God purposely limited the size of his army to a small group of selected men.[84] Gideon sought special signs to prove to himself that this was God's will[85] and, in the end, believed God and accomplished an astonishing victory. He remained faithful to the will of God when his people wanted to make him and his descendants rulers over the land.[86] However, the thought occurred to him that this great victory he had accomplished ought to be remembered. No doubt this was Satan's activity in the mind. The idea seemed so innocent, and God himself had ordered monuments to be made as a remembrance of other victories. What made the difference here, however, was again the will. Gideon's idea might have seemed innocent and based on a past act of the will of God, but in his case it was not the will of God. Satan achieved his work of temptation once

---

82   Isaiah 39:1-7.
83   Judges 6:15.
84   Judges 7:7.
85   Judges 6:37.
86   Judges 8:22.

again. The *ephod* [87] was made to remember a great victory of God. However, it became the cause of a great failure, when the people later fell into idolatry by honoring the ephod.[88]

Mystical Powers

Another weakness that Satan exploits is man's tendency to feel a kind of awe or fear in the face of unexplained phenomenon or mystical powers. This tendency is such a dangerous weakness that Jesus told his disciples that Satan's temptation in this area would *seduce, if it were possible, even the elect.*[89] Entire libraries could be written about the myriad of superstitions that exist and affect people's lives in countries all over the world. That which is mystical seems to have a special attraction to fallen man, and Satan is well aware of this opportunity. The Colossians were being tempted and deceived in this way as we see from Paul's warning to them to *Let no man beguile you of your reward in a voluntary humility and worshipping of angels, intruding into those things which he hath not seen, vainly puffed up by his fleshly mind.*[90]

When Satan tempted Eve, he tried to gain credibility by appearing as a beautiful creature. Many other methods of gaining credibility have been discussed. However, in the process of man's temptation in mystical areas, credibility is often substituted with the power of suggestion. The supernatural is a

---

87 Ephod: something girt, a sacred vestment worn originally by the high priest (Ex 28:4), afterwards by the ordinary priest (1Sa 22:18), and characteristic of his office (1Sa 2:18, 28; 14:3). It was worn by Samuel, and also by David (2Sa 6:14). It was made of fine linen, and consisted of two pieces, which hung from the neck, and covered both the back and front, above the tunic and outer garment (Ex 28:31). That of the high priest was embroidered with divers colours. The two pieces were joined together over the shoulders (hence in Latin called superhumerale) by clasps or buckles of gold or precious stones, and fastened round the waist by a "curious girdle of gold, blue, purple, and fine twined linen" (Ex 28:6-12). *Easton's Bible Dictionary, Power Bible* CD v. 3.7a.

88 Judges 8:27.

89 Mark 13:22.

90 Colossians 2:18.

tremendous force in the minds of men and is especially effective when there is ignorance of the natural forces and processes that God created in the world and universe. Satan has no problem finding someone who will form a false conclusion about an experience related to some unknown phenomenon. He will then use authoritative declarations that become superstitions. At this point, he merely needs to sow the questions in a man's mind: What if this is really true? What if this will really bring me harm? What if this will really bring me protection or well-being? When there is ignorance of truth, whether it be spiritual or natural, the power of these suggestions is even greater. However, even when there is intelligent knowledge of true science and basic spiritual principles, the power of suggestion is still able to cause enough doubt that, against all reason, man will act according to his own will and not according to God's.

Satan's use of the power of suggestion is not limited to mystical things. He commonly uses this deceitful device to win the struggle for man's will in areas such as health. A great many physical maladies are not based on any true defect but rather on the mind's fabrication as a result of the power of suggestion.

Still another area that is susceptible to the power of suggestion is that of child discipline. Satan has used philosophers, psychologists, or friends and relatives to come up with all sorts of suggestions to sow in parents' minds. These suggestions play on both their deep feelings of affection and concern for their children. Their strong desire for social acceptance causes them to disregard God's teachings in this area and act according to their own will.

Accusations

Somewhat related to Satan's use of the power of suggestion is his practice of being the *accuser of our brethren*.[91] He maliciously

---

91   Revelation 12:10.

imitates the conscience of man, making him feel accused of every failure and disobedience possible. The weakness of the flesh gives him plenty of material to use in his accusations, and he leads the mind to think that the flesh is the true personality, obscuring the reality of the new nature. Satan even torments man by causing him to feel imagined sin. As we will see in the following section, the conscience is capable of becoming sensitive to traditions, customs, and feelings about right and wrong just as it is to scriptural right and wrong. This gives Satan even more material to work with. He can accuse and worry man about things that are not even actual disobedience, because he knows some people will simply feel guilty.

If a Christian is not aware of the origin of these accusations and focuses his attention on his weaknesses and sins, he may come to believe that there is no hope for him of ever living the way he knows he should. This can lead him to despair if he has a somewhat sensitive conscience. He will relate this experience to his personal value before God and man and be tormented by the feeling of worthlessness.

Satan does this first of all because he is evil, malicious, and hateful. He delights in tormenting and destroying. Obscuring God's grace, mercy, and goodness brings him satisfaction and causes man to dwell on evil, failure, and pain. He tries to make God's work of grace in man appear as a failure by pointing out the wickedness of the flesh. He knows that the effect of his accusations may cause man to have a defeated, sorrowful spirit. In this way, his accusations are another example of the power of suggestion.

The result that Satan desires from causing a sorrowful spirit in man is, again, the control of the will. John Bunyan's description of Christian in the "Slough of Despond"[92] illustrates the

---

92   Bunyan, *Pilgrim's Progress,* 20-21.

inability of the will of man to help himself when he is overcome by the sorrow of worthlessness and defeat.

Jerry and Kirsti Newcombe mention this tactic of Satan, saying: "The devil lies to us at two ends of the spectrum. Before we sin, he gives the line about how just this one little time won't hurt. After we sin, he tries to convince us that we can't get up again or give up the sin or that God won't forgive us or that He won't ever use us again."[93]

Nehemiah warned the people of Jerusalem of the weakness of this sorrowful spirit, saying: *neither be ye sorry,* (sorrowful) *for the joy of the Lord is your strength.*[94] He recognized that this trap of Satan would weaken them in a time when they had to be especially strong and countered the thoughts and tendency to despair with the truth of the joy of the Lord.

So effective is this trap that even when one comes into the presence of God in prayer, he may feel defeated and discouraged. This is not what the Holy Spirit desires to produce in man. The Holy Spirit may cause him to feel sorrow for sin and disgust for evil, but he will magnify the work of Christ for relief from sin and defeat, which will bring joy to the soul as he focuses on the glory and goodness of God. If there is no relief from this sorrowful spirit, even before God in prayer, something is wrong, and this is an attack of the accuser and not the conviction of the Spirit.

Even when a Christian resists these accusations by remembering his justification through the shed blood of Christ, Satan does not give up easily. He will usually feign defeat but comes back with another attack.

Distortion of Obedience or Faith

A Christian's power over temptation is his true, spiritual faith

---

93   Newcombe, *A Way of Escape,* 6.
94   Nehemiah 8:10.

in God.[95] Trusting God will cause a sense of rest from struggle but will not conflict with obedience. Faith and obedience are either inseparable or they are vain.

Owen says, "We must perform our duties in faith, deriving our strength from Christ, without whom we *can do nothing* (John 15:5). It is not enough to believe, though that is necessary in every good work (Ephesians 2:10). Faith must characterize our obedience."[96]

Obedience that does not result from faith will be fulfilled in man's own power and by his own will. This is not only unacceptable to God, it is vanity and unable *to stand against the wiles of the devil.*[97] On the other hand, *faith without works is dead.*[98] That is faith as a concept and not true, spiritual faith. Faith without works will result in weakness as it is founded on man's will and not God's. The divine combination of faith and obedience is not always clear to a Christian, and Satan knows how to play this against him.

When the Christian rests in Christ, accepts his forgiveness, and decides to trust in his grace and power, Satan causes him to fear that this is in conflict with personal discipline and will result in license to sin. If Satan can make the Christian worry about resting in God's grace and power more than he is "supposed to," he may be able to get the Christian's mind off of the power of God and so focused on his struggle against sin that he will begin to struggle according to his own power and will. Worry or fear that there is a point where one can depend too much on faith in God's power and grace comes from Satan's distortions of scriptural truths such as Jude's warning about ungodly men subtly *turning the grace of our God into lasciviousness.*[99]

95   1 John 5:4 *For whatsoever is born of God overcometh the world: and this is the victory that overcometh the world, even our faith.*

96   Owen, *Sin and Temptation*, 55.

97   Ephesians 6:11.

98   James 2:26.

99   Jude 1:4.

The current struggle in the Presbyterian and Anglican Churches over the ordination of homosexual ministers is an example of this problem. However, Satan not only tries to create that extreme distortion of grace, he also uses some Christians' fear and disgust to drive them to the opposite extreme. "Grace" becomes suspect, the scriptural concept of liberty is avoided, and Christianity becomes a pharisaical system of standards, traditions, methods, and issues. Even the eternal security of salvation through faith in the finished work of Christ on the cross is feared as a weakness that could result in Christians feeling that it is acceptable to sin. This focus on man's duty and righteousness can appear as piety, but if the true faith of resting in Christ's work and living through his power is not the foundation, the piety has degenerated to mere religiousness. Paul indirectly described this real possibility when he said that tongues, prophecy, and faith without the active obedience of love are nothing, and good works without love, which is by faith, are nothing.[100]

On the other hand, Satan can use the feeling of emptiness that many experience in strict, tradition-centered, superficial Christianity to drive them to seek some "deeper" spiritual experience. He distorts important biblical truths and offers such remedies as emotional experience or the joy of liberty. For some, he tries to convince them that emotionalism and "supernatural" experiences will fill their sense of emptiness. For others, he casts the blame on standards and duty as the reason for their feeling of emptiness. They focus on their liberty to a point where they become defensive and irritated by legalistic Christianity. They show off their liberty by going against common standards in which Christianity has been identified to the point of being worldly and scoffing at Christians who walk in a proper balance of faith and obedience. If Satan can cause an

---

100   1 Corinthians 13:1-3.

out-of-proportion focus on either faith or obedience instead of the correct, divine combination of both, he will have caused the Christian to act according to his own will, which is the victory he seeks. Once he causes this willfulness in Christianity, he has achieved *a form of godliness* but without the power[101] and has freedom to continue tempting in all of his other subtle ways.

In summary, we have seen that Satan's desire is to cause man to act according to his own will and not in submission to the will of God. To most effectively accomplish this task, he works in obscurity, remaining unnoticed, and in that way avoids detection and resistance. The mind is his workshop. He uses the easy access to the subconscious mind to sow corruption, fear, anger, and other imaginations that will prepare the mind for his subtle attack on the conscious area of the mind. In the conscious mind, he distorts truth and attempts to lead the mind to form false conclusions, which exert a great power over the will. He uses tactics of deceit to cause these false conclusions, which include gaining credibility, showing concern (which also casts doubt on God's motives), and giving expert, authoritative declarations. These tactics are applied specifically to areas that are particular stumbling blocks in each individual's life. Other tactics include using the power of suggestion, accusations, and a distortion of the divine balance of obedience and faith.

Throughout this process of temptation, Satan achieves different levels of victory. The superficial, preparatory levels relate to his work of using natural curiosity, the weakness of the flesh, and the influence of the world to attract and deceive man into forming false conclusions. If Satan can achieve victory at this level, he sometimes attempts to gain victory at a deeper level by using these conclusions to cause obsessions (which have been discussed previously) for certain desires or purposes that become a supposed basis or necessity for man's satisfaction.

---

101   2 Timothy 3:5.

Intents of the Heart

The deepest level of victory that Satan can achieve is in the area of the *intents of the heart*.[102] At this point, man has formed false conclusions. In some cases, he may be obsessed with a desire. Finally, he plans to act according to his own will, even consciously knowing it is against God's will. At some point in Eve's temptation, she planned to eat the forbidden fruit. She was not ignorant of God's will but had put it in the back of her mind where it was not her guiding light. She had not taken the fruit yet, but she intended to do so. The purpose had been sown in her will. The will still had to decide to take the fruit, but the intention to do so was already there.

When a person gets to the place of having formed intentions to sin, he is in grave danger. Whether or not these intentions can be reversed is debatable and a question for much reflection. In a sense, the will can still decide not to sin, and in many cases God can intervene and make it impossible to fulfill some intention. God does not actually violate the freedom of the will, however, and in most cases intentions so dominate the will that Satan's work is done and his purpose has been achieved. Realistically, to thwart Satan's work, he must be resisted at some previous level of temptation, as we will discuss later.

---

102 Hebrews 4:12.

CHAPTER 6

The Conscience

Frequently I have mentioned man's conscience, which God uses to convict him of right and wrong and which Satan tries to either dull or imitate and confuse. Having discussed the abundance of factors involved in temptation and looking forward to the discussion of the many factors involved in overcoming temptation, a more in-depth study of the conscience is appropriate and needful at this point. The conscience is a pivotal point between the wrong that Satan desires to cause through temptation and the right that God desires to manifest even in the face of temptation.

Webster's most basic definition of conscience is "Internal or self-knowledge, or judgment of right and wrong; or the faculty, power or principle within us, which decides on the lawfulness or unlawfulness of our own actions and affections, and instantly approves or condemns them."[103] He also cites a portion of John 8:9 which says, *And they which heard it, being convicted by their own conscience went out one by one.*

This passage is one example of the force of conscience in action. The scribes and Pharisees brought to Jesus a woman who was caught in the very act of adultery. They were seeking to destroy the influence that he had among the people and so told him, *Now Moses in the law commanded us, that such should be stoned: but what sayest thou?*[104] Jesus, of course, had the ability and the right to make a clear judgment in this case, but that was

103   Webster, *American Dictionary.*
104   John 8:5.

not the real point in question. The real point was the hypocrisy of these men using the divine law of God to accomplish the evil deed of accusing and slandering Christ. For this reason, Jesus did not play their game but rather turned the situation right back on them. After they continued to pressure him, *he lifted up himself, and said unto them, he that is without sin among you, let him first cast a stone at her.*[105] What the scribes and Pharisees had to face at this point was their own conscience on public display. The power of conscience was effective enough to change their will, and they left.

In other cases, the conscience is not effective. The conscience of the men of Shechem was so dull that they conspired with Abimelech and murdered Gideon's sons in order to obtain power even after Gideon by faith in God, against overwhelming odds, freed Israel from bondage to the Midianites.[106] Jezebel and the men she bribed to witness falsely against Naboth and have that innocent man killed is another example.[107] Likewise, the story of how Joash was protected from death and made king by Jehoiada only to later have Jehoiada's own son killed also shows an ineffective conscience.[108]

Why the conscience fulfills its purpose in some cases and does not in others is of great concern in understanding and overcoming temptation. Four different states of the conscience are either referred to directly or illustrated in Scripture. These are: The correct state or sensitive conscience, and the incorrect states of a weak, seared, or dead conscience. The following scale of the four states of the conscience can help to understand and study what each is and how it relates to the others.

---

105 John 8:7.
106 Judges 9:1-6.
107 1 Kings 21:4-14.
108 2 Chronicles 23:1-21; 24:20-22.

Scale of Conscience

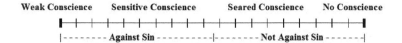

Weak Conscience   Sensitive Conscience   Seared Conscience   No Conscience

|- - - - - - - - Against Sin - - - - - - - - - -|- - - - - - - Not Against Sin - - - - - -|

Sensitive Conscience

When the conscience is functioning the way it was created to work and is capable of judging right and wrong, "deciding on the lawfulness or unlawfulness of our own actions and affections and instantly approving or condemning them" it is a sensitive conscience. By "sensitive," I mean it will react clearly and correctly to each stimulation of actions, words, thoughts, or attitudes. This has been compared in a useful way to a well-tuned instrument. When stretched and tuned, a guitar string will give a clear, distinguished response to a stimulus. As it loses tension, the response changes until it becomes dull and finally gives no response at all. A sensitive conscience will have the capability of discerning right and wrong and will quickly convict of sin. When the mind is in its subconscious state of activity and Satan begins his tactic of leading it to sinful imaginations, the conscience is capable of detecting wrong and waking the mind up to be aware of Satan's activity. It can then eliminate the wrong thoughts.

Paul demonstrated the importance of the conscience by his earnest interest in having a public testimony that would be acceptable to the conscience of others. This desire was expressed in 2 Corinthians 4:2, *But have renounced the hidden things of dishonesty, not walking in craftiness, nor handling the word of God deceitfully; but by manifestation of the truth commending ourselves to every man's conscience in the sight of God* and was repeated in 2 Corinthians 5:11, *Knowing therefore the terror of the Lord, we persuade men; but we are made manifest unto God;*

and I trust also are made manifest in your consciences. He also demonstrated the importance of the conscience by establishing it as one of the prime foundations of his own credibility before others, saying: *I say the truth in Christ, I lie not, my conscience also bearing me witness in the Holy Ghost.*[109]

The mind, emotions, and will are all affected by the conscience. Conviction of sin by the conscience is clarified by the mind's capability to reason why. If the mind has the knowledge of right and wrong, it will confirm and clarify the actions of the conscience.

Owen comments on this subject, "In addition, because the mind works spiritually in the soul it needs to be stirred and enlightened. The conscience is not apt to be aroused if the mind fails to warn the soul."[110]

On the other hand, the knowledge of the mind can determine the sensitivity of the conscience in many cases. As a child, I remember hearing a new Christian lady compliment my father after church, saying: "preacher, that was a h*ll of a good sermon." That compliment raised a lot of eyebrows, and rightly so as it demonstrated a lack of conscience in regards to proper vocabulary. However, no one doubted the sincerity of the compliment, but all understood that this new Christian simply did not yet have the spiritual knowledge needed to have a sensitive conscience in the area of her vocabulary. I am sure that in a short time she increased in spiritual knowledge of right and wrong according to the Bible, and her conscience was soon awakened and became sensitive in the area of her vocabulary.

Knowledge of the foundational principles of right and wrong will have a great deal to do with the conscience. The more correct knowledge the mind has of right and wrong, the more sensitive the conscience will be. The greater the ignorance of

---

109   Romans 9:1.
110   Owen, *Sin and Temptation,* 52.

right and wrong, the less functional the conscience will be. As a person grows in knowledge of right and wrong according to the Word of God, he also increases in sensitivity of conscience. This knowledge of right and wrong must be according to the Word of God. If knowledge of right and wrong is based on an incorrect source or authority, there will be a corresponding increase in incorrect sensitivity, and things may not be correctly judged. (This weak state will be discussed in depth later.)

However, both scriptural evidence and observation of society show that a certain amount of knowledge of right and wrong is inherent in man. Even where the Word of God is not commonly taught, a certain degree of law and order exists that is based on biblical principles. The apostle Paul used this truth to demonstrate the fallacy of the self-righteous Jews' attitude of being superior to the Gentiles simply because as a nation they had received the revelations of the Word of God. He told them, *For when the Gentiles, which have not the law, do by nature the things contained in the law, these, having not the law, are a law unto themselves: Which shew the work of the law written in their hearts, their conscience also bearing witness, and their thoughts the mean while accusing or else excusing one another.*[111] This seems to coincide with John 1:9 which mentions the *true Light which lighteth every man that cometh into the world.*

The conscience, then, has a certain ability to discern right and wrong even without the direct knowledge of the Word of God. For this reason, Paul could say of the unbelieving pagan world, *Because that which may be known of God is manifest in them; for God hath shewed it unto them. For the invisible things of him from the creation of the world are clearly seen, being understood by the things that are made, even his eternal power and Godhead; so that they are without excuse.*[112] David had also

---

111 Romans 2:14-15.
112 Romans 1:19-20.

stated this principle in Psalm 19:1, saying: *the heavens declare the glory of God; and the firmament showeth his handiwork.* This degree of sensitivity of conscience in man is enough to guide him to seek a greater knowledge of right and wrong through the Word of God. It is limited in itself, however, and will lose its sensitivity when it is disregarded by the will.

Just as the conscience interacts with the mind, it also inter-acts with the emotions. When the conscience is "clear" or has been followed through obedience, repentance or the asking of forgiveness, an emotional response of peace, satisfaction, and even joy, is common. This state of the conscience is referred to by Paul as being a "good" conscience and was one of his own primary goals as a Christian as well as one of the primary goals he set for others. Speaking to the Jews of his own testimony he said, *Men and brethren, I have lived in all good conscience before God until this day.*[113] Later he exhorted Timothy, *Now the end of the commandment is charity out of a pure heart, and of a good conscience, and of faith unfeigned.*[114] Hebrews 13:18 also uses the term "good" when referring to a clear conscience, saying: *Pray for us: for we trust we have a good conscience, in all things willing to live honestly,* and also Peter described a clear conscience in the same way when he instructed the readers of his epistle, *Having a good conscience; that, whereas they speak evil of you, as of evildoers, they may be ashamed that falsely accuse your good conversation in Christ.*[115]

A clear conscience is one of the most emotionally comfort-able and enjoyable experiences in man's life. Paul wrote of this joy in relation to a clear conscience in 2 Corinthians 1:12, *For our rejoicing is this, the testimony of our conscience, that in sim-plicity and godly sincerity, not with fleshly wisdom, but by the*

---

113   Acts 23:1.
114   1 Timothy 1:5.
115   1 Peter 3:16.

grace of God, we have had our conversation in the world, and more abundantly to you-ward. This joy is evident when man experiences the change from a violated conscience to a clear conscience through the act of repentance or the asking of forgiveness. In that moment, the comfort of a clear conscience is cherished when compared to what is felt when it was violated. Comfort may be taken for granted when the conscience has not been violated and no forgiveness is necessary.

When the conscience is disregarded and violated by the will, there are natural resulting emotions of guilt and shame. These emotions are uncomfortable and are a powerful motivation for change. Everyone has experienced this sensation of conviction, and Scripture contains innumerable examples. Adam and Eve experienced the very first negative emotions when they sinned. Their distress and shame caused them to attempt to cover their nakedness with fig leaves and try to hide from God.[116] Joseph's brothers had also been carrying around the guilt and shame of having sold him into slavery and grieved the heart of their father with the lie about his death. Even after thirteen years, the first thing that came to their minds when they were faced with the fear of punishment in Egypt was their guilt over Joseph.[117] The story of the Samarian lepers also illustrates this action of the conscience. Second Kings 7:8-9 says:

> *And when these lepers came to the uttermost part*
> *of the camp, they went into one tent, and did eat*
> *and drink, and carried thence silver, and gold, and*
> *raiment, and went and hid it; and came again, and*
> *entered into another tent, and carried thence also,*
> *and went and hid it. Then they said one to another,*
> *We do not well: this day is a day of good tidings, and*
> *we hold our peace: if we tarry till the morning light,*

---

116   Genesis 3:7-8.
117   Genesis 42:21; 44:16.

some mischief will come upon us: now therefore
come, that we may go and tell the king's household.

This conviction produced by the conscience has already been mentioned in the story of the Pharisees who brought the woman taken in adultery to Jesus, and it is even seen in Judas Iscariot who betrayed Jesus in Matthew 27:3: *Then Judas, which had betrayed him, when he saw that he was condemned, repented himself, and brought again the thirty pieces of silver to the chief priests and elders.* John also spoke of the guilt and shame of conviction, saying: *For if our heart condemn us, God is greater than our heart, and knoweth all things.*[118]

The correct change is to repent and gain a clear conscience. The will is capable, however, of ignoring the shame, and the mind can help in disregarding the emotions by reasoning them away with false conclusions. The practice of disregarding the conscience will diminish the emotions of guilt and shame but will not replace them with the joy of peace and satisfaction.

This demonstrates the relation of the conscience to the will. The free will of man has the final say. God has given man a conscience to detect temptation and expose it as wrong so it can be resisted and overcome. The mind is capable of strengthening the influence of the conscience as it increases in the knowledge of right and wrong through the Word of God. The joy, peace, and satisfaction experienced when the conscience is followed are powerful influences to motivate the will to obey the conscience. This power is even seen in the case of Job who, in spite of his suffering and confusion, declared, *My righteousness I hold fast, and will not let it go: my heart shall not reproach me so long as I live.*[119] Paul also showed how the will is motivated by the conscience saying in Acts 24:16, *And herein do I exercise*

---

118   1 John 3:20.
119   Job 27:6.

myself, to have always a conscience void of offence toward God, and toward men."

The extreme discomfort caused by guilt and shame increase this motivation. On the other hand, the weakness of the flesh, the attraction of the world, and the deceit of Satan are powerful motivations for the will to surrender to temptation and violate the conscience. It follows then, that when the conscience is sensitive, there will be a struggle. The natural appetites will be incited by Satan to desire fulfillment according to their fleshly, fallen condition. The sensitive conscience will detect the wrong of this desire and cause the mind and emotions to recognize and feel that wrong. If a person has "developed appetites" from a time previous to the awakening of a sensitive conscience, he may have a struggle in those areas. In the end, the will must have the last word and make the final decision and becomes the key to understanding and overcoming temptation. This again demonstrates why the will is the "prize" that is sought in the spiritual warfare between God and Satan.

Weak Conscience

Getting back to our scale of conscience, we see that the "weak" state of the conscience is placed to the left of the correct, sensitive state. (See page 79) This is because it is an extreme and is not how God designed the conscience to be.

As mentioned before, in order to function correctly, the conscience depends upon the correct source of knowledge of right and wrong, which is the Word of God. If this source is incorrect, a person may have a sensitive conscience, but it might react to circumstances that are not condemned by God as wrong. This is the essence of what the Bible calls "a weak conscience."

A person's criteria of right and wrong can be based upon many things. His religious practices will be the single most influential factor in these criteria. Many of the world's religions do not accept the Bible as the Word of God and teach doctrines of other men who are accepted as prophets. In this condition, a person with a sensitive conscience will react negatively to many things that are not sins against God. Other religions add teachings to the Word of God, which has the same effect. Some religions take away from the Word of God and leave the conscience without complete criteria. Our most common experience in this area is with people who simply misunderstand the Word of God.

With an incorrect source of knowledge of right and wrong, a person might feel convicted of sin for something that is not truly sin. This person feels condemned by practices that are not condemned by God. This "imagined evil" can also be based on one's culture. Standards of modesty and appearance vary from culture to culture. If people from these different cultures accept their standards as the criteria of right and wrong, a different reaction of the conscience appears in each culture.

The traditions of different cultures are related to standards. These can also vary and will result in a great difference of how the conscience will react from culture to culture. Even individual families can develop their own standards and traditions and consider them part of the criteria of right and wrong. Many times these standards and traditions are incorporated into religions, causing the conscience to react to them as well as to the Word of God. If these standards and traditions are taught by preachers, teachers, or parents, and the hearers accept the teachings as being equal with the Bible, this weak state of the conscience will spread to others. Paul was aware of this, and his desire that all men would form the correct, biblical criteria for their conscience was demonstrated when he spoke of how noble the Bereans were because they *searched the Scriptures daily whether those things were so.*[120] Sadly, many preachers, teachers,

---

120   Acts 17:11.

and parents do not have this desire but prefer their criteria be accepted without question or comparison to the Word of God.

This demonstrates to us how important it is to study the Bible thoroughly. We must meditate sincerely upon its teachings and maintain the correct attitude of desiring to discern God's perfect criteria as the foundation to which the conscience will be sensitive. One must compare what affects his conscience with biblical teachings, examples, and the Spirit of Christ and be willing to accept the possibility of having formed incorrect criteria that is not conformed to the Word of God. It is possible to have correct, biblical criteria in one area of life and have incorrect criteria in another area. One neither justifies nor negates the other. The correct criteria, based on the Word of God, must be developed in each area of life and experience in order to eliminate the possibility of a weak conscience.

In our study of a weak conscience, we need to see how this relates to temptation. A weak conscience does have the sensitivity that God intended. However, the person is exposed to the temptation of violating his conscience in two different ways. The first way is obvious. A person can violate his conscience by falling to the temptation of doing something that is against his criteria of right and wrong. The second way is not so obvious. A person with a weak conscience can violate his conscience by following the example of another person who has a correct conscience. It is interesting and of great importance to notice that when the Bible mentions the weak conscience, it is in relation to this type of temptation.

Paul dealt with this problem when writing to the Corinthians and Romans. The issue of that day was about meat sacrificed to idols. Some Christians, including the apostle Paul, had the correct, biblical knowledge that idols were merely objects and there is only one true God over all.[121] These Christians could eat meat that

---

121   1 Corinthians 8:4-6.

had been sacrificed to idols without any condemnation of their conscience because of this clear knowledge. Other Christians, however, had the idea that eating meat sacrificed to idols was a form of idolatry, and their conscience forbade them to eat it. The Bible says that these Christians had a weak conscience.[122] What is extremely interesting and important is God's attitude toward this circumstance. The point of Paul's teachings was not to demonstrate the weakness of some Christians' consciences and much less to condemn them. Rather, what was important was that even the weak conscience must not be violated. Christians with a clear knowledge of God and of his will in the matter were exhorted not to be a stumbling block to those who had a weak conscience, even if this included sacrificing their own personal liberty. They were told that if they ate this meat knowingly, in the presence of a Christian with a weak conscience, that Christian might follow their example and eat the meat in violation of his own conscience.[123] Paul used strong words to express the importance of Christians taking this responsibility toward other Christians with a weak conscience, saying: *And through thy knowledge shall the weak brother perish, for whom Christ died? But when ye sin so against the brethren, and wound their weak conscience, ye sin against Christ. Wherefore, if meat make my brother to offend, I will eat no flesh while the world standeth, lest I make my brother to offend.*[124]

This should open our eyes to how important the sensitivity of the conscience is to God. The sensitivity of the conscience is what is at stake here. Even if a Christian with a weak conscience does not actually sin, when he violates his conscience, a damaging consequence of a decrease in sensitivity occurs. As the conscience decreases in sensitivity, there is less and less

---

122 1 Corinthians 8:7.
123 1 Corinthians 8:8-10.
124 1 Corinthians 8:11-13.

protection from temptation. The principle to understand is that a weak conscience can be corrected through the enlightenment of greater biblical knowledge, but it must not be violated. Sensitivity of the conscience can be directed but must not be diminished.[125]

The following graph pictures the relation of conscience to self-control. It illustrates how the natural level of conscience that is inherent in man can be increased or decreased according to his increase in knowledge of truth and his response of disciplining himself to follow the direction of his conscience or, on the contrary, of violating the direction of the conscience.

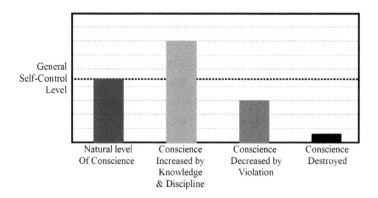

Knowledge Violation & Discipline

As the mind increases in knowledge of truth and the conscience is obeyed, a corresponding increase in self-control takes place. Any act of obedience to the direction of the conscience will produce a general increase in self-control that can show up in all areas of life. For instance, if a person follows his conscience and learns to tell the truth, this person will develop a greater ability to resist other temptations, such as stealing or sensual activities.

On the other hand, if the conscience is violated in any one

125   1 Corinthians 10:23-33; Romans 14.

area of temptation, a corresponding weakness will develop that will hinder the person's ability to resist temptation in all other areas of life.

Owen warns, "Repeated acts of the will to sin often produce a disposition and inclination toward sin. This proneness leads to easy consent. We must exercise great care to watch against such a condition in our soul."[126]

If a person violates his conscience in the area of telling the truth, he will experience a corresponding loss of self-control in other temptations such as stealing or sensual activity. This demonstrates the necessity to keep the conscience in "fine tune" in all areas of life. If children and young people are not trained to have a sensitive conscience and obey its direction, even simple selfishness that appears to be only bothersome will eventually affect their ability to resist other temptations with more drastic consequences. The conscience may be violated in regards to gluttony with the excuse that it is not hurting anyone and is not a moral problem. However, if there is knowledge of wrong and the conscience is violated when convicted of this wrong, then a weakening effect occurs on the person's self-control that could also lead to moral failure. As mentioned earlier, the attitude that pornography is simply a matter of personal preference and does not affect others is an idea that is destroyed by the knowledge of the global effect on self-control when the conscience is violated in any area. Drug trafficking and even violent crimes of rape and murder can often be traced to earlier violations of the conscience in areas of pornography or "socially acceptable" sins that destroyed the person's conscience of wrong and, in turn, his self-control.

Seared Conscience
We can see then that as the conscience is violated by a direct

126 Owen, *Sin and Temptation*, 66.

act of the will, sensitivity will decrease. This state of decreased sensitivity of the conscience is the third area of our scale and is called a seared conscience. Paul described people in this condition to Timothy, saying: *Speaking lies in hypocrisy; having their conscience seared with a hot iron* (1 Tim. 4:2). He expressed the same in Titus 1:15, *Unto the pure all things are pure: but unto them that are defiled and unbelieving is nothing pure; but even their mind and conscience is defiled.*

Recognizing the danger of acting against the conscience is another motivation to resist temptation as the conscience directs. The consequence of disregarding the direction of the conscience is not only the corruption of *sowing to the flesh* but also of losing the sensitivity of the conscience that is so necessary for victory and the abundant life that is reaped from *sowing to the spirit.*[127] Once again, the will is the key. All other influences that stimulate the conscience will only cause a clear strong reaction indicating right or wrong. However, the will actually affects the quality and functionality of the conscience. When the will acts according to the direction of the conscience, it is kept in "fine-tune." When the will disregards the conscience and acts against its direction, the fine-tuning is lost, the string is loosened, and it finally gives no indication at all.

This is probably the widest area on the scale. At first, acting against the conscience is sufficient because of the guilt and shame that result. These terribly uncomfortable emotions often cause one to repent and act again according to his conscience which, in turn, brings back the "fine-tuning." However, as it becomes more common for a person to violate his conscience, and patterns or habits begin to form, it becomes easier and easier to disregard the conscience as the guilt and shame become less and less potent. This can be illustrated by placing this "Shame Factor" in our Scale of Conscience diagram.

---

127 Galatians 6:8.

Scale of Conscience

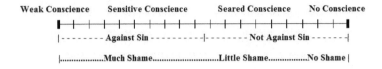

We see how the amount of shame that one feels toward sin relates to the scale of conscience and one's resistance to temptation.

During this process of disregarding the conscience more often, the will resorts to the mind to reason away the guilt and shame. Jeremiah described this process in the lives of the people of Israel. In Jeremiah 2:19, he speaks of the conviction of the conscience, saying: *Thine own wickedness shall correct thee, and thy backslidings shall reprove thee: know therefore and see that it is an evil thing and bitter, that thou hast forsaken the LORD thy God, and that my fear is not in thee, saith the Lord GOD of hosts.* Israel, however, disregarded this conviction of conscience, and is likened to the stubbornness of a wild donkey in verse 24: *A wild ass used to the wilderness, that snuffeth up the wind at her pleasure; in her occasion who can turn her away? All they that seek her will not weary themselves; in her month they shall find her.*

The next verse, verse 25, speaks of the process of the mind making excuses for not resisting temptation: *Withhold thy foot from being unshod, and thy throat from thirst: but thou saidst, There is no hope: no; for I have loved strangers, and after them will I go.* One of the most common excuses used to reason away the lack of regard for the conviction of the conscience is "I don't have the strength to resist" or "There is no hope." These tricks in the mind are used to alleviate the guilt and make it easier on the will to act against the conscience.

The next step of feeling shame is mentioned in verse 26: *As the thief is ashamed when he is found, so is the house of Israel ashamed; they, their kings, their princes, and their priests, and their prophets.* As the shame was eliminated by reasoning instead of by repentance, their consciences became more and more dull until they were capable of accepting behavior that before would not only have been considered sinful, but foolish. Jeremiah described this condition in verses 27 to 28: *Saying to a stock, Thou art my father; and to a stone, Thou hast brought me forth: for they have turned their back unto me, and not their face: but in the time of their trouble they will say, Arise, and save us. But where are thy gods that thou hast made thee? Let them arise, if they can save thee in the time of thy trouble: for according to the number of thy cities are thy gods, O Judah.* Finally, as this process of disobedience and reasoning away the guilt and shame continued, their consciences became seared to the point that not even punishment could affect their will, as shown in verse 30: *In vain have I smitten your children; they received no correction: your own sword hath devoured your prophets, like a destroying lion.*

During the process of the gradual searing of the conscience, change is still possible. Great change is either sudden or gradual through the regeneration of the spirit in salvation, as we read in Hebrews 9:14: *How much more shall the blood of Christ, who through the eternal Spirit offered himself without spot to God, purge your conscience from dead works to serve the living God?* For those who are believers but are forming habits that slowly diminish the sensitivity of the conscience, there can still be the experience of *the renewing of your mind.*[128] Hebrews 10:22 also mentions this change in the conscience, saying: *Let us draw near with a true heart in full assurance of faith, having our hearts sprinkled from an evil conscience, and our bodies washed with pure water.* God uses many things to effect this change. The

128 Romans 12:2.

Holy Spirit may directly work on the mind and heart to convince man of sin, the terror of judgment, and the only escape through repentance. Other times God uses tragedies and trials to open the eyes of man, break up the routines that are forming sinful habits, and break the barriers of his will. The emptiness that results from seeking satisfaction apart from God's will is a powerful force for change. Sometimes a Spirit-filled parent, preacher, or layman may give a particularly strong or personal exhortation to whatever conscience still remains in a person, which may bring him to an understanding of the truth and to the freedom that follows. Children and other "tender spots" are often the cause of a reawakening of the conviction of the conscience. If these opportunities are not heeded, however, the opposite effect will occur, and the searing of the conscience will be even greater

The condition of the conscience after this process is said to be "seared." This biblical analogy gives the image of a brand that both deadens the flesh till there is no feeling and identifies the person with those who can sin with no feeling at all.

Stanley speaks of the seriousness of this danger, saying: "Another reason you must once again take seriously those areas of your life you have allowed to slip is that choosing not to deal with sin ultimately leads to what Scripture calls a hard heart. A hard heart develops when people hear the truth, believe the truth, but refuse to apply the truth. Developing a hard heart is a process that takes time. But each time Christians recognize sin in their lives, feel convicted, and yet do nothing about it, they become less and less sensitive to the promptings of the Holy Spirit. Finally, they reach the point where they feel no conviction at all over particular sins. They become callous, and they quench the Spirit in their lives (1 Thess. 5:19), which is a dangerous thing to do."[129]

---

129   Stanley, *Winning the War Within,* 13.

Dead Conscience

We come to the final area on the scale of conscience that is the extreme case of being lost altogether or dead. Guilt and shame are no longer felt, so there is no discomfort in sin. Sensitivity is no longer related to right and wrong but rather to the unguided mind and emotions, *having the understanding darkened, being alienated from the life of God through the ignorance that is in them, because of the blindness of their heart.*[130] Without any conscience to convict of right and wrong, the unbridled emotions of the corrupt flesh will take control of the will, and right or wrong becomes a concept associated with like or dislike, convenience or inconvenience, gain or loss. The mind is void of conscience of truth and can and will lie to itself easily and habitually with excuses and reasonings that defend the flesh to the point of being irrational.[131] The will is now dominated by the flesh. They are *servants of corruption*[132] and unrestrained in regards to selfishness, egotism, and sin. No struggle is felt in the heart against wrong, but rather only a struggle to have satisfaction and fulfillment of desires. The natural appetites enslave the will for the purpose of self-gratification. There is no resistance of the will to the formation of developed appetites, so the most deviant behavior is not only practiced but defended as if it were natural and acceptable. A desire to flaunt this deviant behavior increases, and a struggle for political power and the right to not only live in this corruption but to teach it and force it on others. The apostle Paul described this process of increasing degeneration with no conscience in Romans 1:21-32:

> *Because that, when they knew God, they glorified him not as God, neither were thankful; but became vain in their imaginations, and their foolish heart*

---

130 Ephesians 4:17-18.
131 2 Peter 2:12; Jude 1:10.
132 2 Peter 2:19.

was darkened. Professing themselves to be wise, they became fools, And changed the glory of the uncorruptible God into an image made like to corruptible man, and to birds, and fourfooted beasts, and creeping things. Wherefore God also gave them up to uncleanness through the lusts of their own hearts, to dishonour their own bodies between themselves: Who changed the truth of God into a lie, and worshipped and served the creature more than the Creator, who is blessed for ever. Amen. For this cause God gave them up unto vile affections: for even their women did change the natural use into that which is against nature: And likewise also the men, leaving the natural use of the woman, burned in their lust one toward another; men with men working that which is unseemly, and receiving in themselves that recompence of their error which was meet. And even as they did not like to retain God in their knowledge, God gave them over to a reprobate mind, to do those things which are not convenient; Being filled with all unrighteousness, fornication, wickedness, covetousness, maliciousness; full of envy, murder, debate, deceit, malignity; whisperers, Backbiters, haters of God, despiteful, proud, boasters, inventors of evil things, disobedient to parents, Without understanding, covenant breakers, without natural affection, implacable, unmerciful: Who knowing the judgment of God, that they which commit such things are worthy of death, not only do the same, but have pleasure in them that do them.

The extreme condition of having a dead conscience leads to a continual lust for even greater extremes in all areas of life associated with satisfaction. Music degenerates into a competition to produce the most unnatural, offensive, loud, vile sounds possible. Money and power are sought through ever greater dishonesty, and even violence. The ability to take advantage or dominate other people in finances or politics becomes a matter of pride and laughter. Life itself has no value so abortion, euthanasia, and murder are explained away as rights, acts of compassion, and understandable results of social injustices. Philosophies go to extremes to where man's place of honor in God's creation is reversed, and he is considered a threat to the well-being of plants, animals, or even insects. The life of unintelligent plants and animals becomes more important than the life of human beings.

Philosophies of law and justice degenerate to having more emotional reactions to the plight of criminals than to the suffering of their victims. True justice is substituted with a vague, circumstantial, convenience-oriented system of supposed "human rights." Even religion degenerates further and further into a mere justification of philosophies and even deviant behavior. Albert Barnes described the past forms of this degeneration of religion in his commentary on 1 Timothy 4:2:

"Such a conscience exists in a mind that will practise delusion without concern; that will carry on a vast system of fraud without wincing; that will incarcerate, scourge, or burn the innocent without compassion; and that will practise gross enormities, and indulge in sensual gratifications under the mask of piety. While there are many eminent exceptions to an application of this to the Papal communion, yet this description will apply better to the Roman priesthood in the time of Luther – found in many other periods of the world – than to any other 'body of men' that ever lived."[133]

Modern day involvement of religion in communism and

---

133 *Albert Barnes Commentary* (*Power Bible* CD, version 2.8).

terrorism and the practice of sanctioning homosexual marriages and even ordinations carries this degeneration to even
further extremes. Jesus told his disciples and all of his faithful
followers that the day will come when *They shall put you out*
of the synagogues: yea, the time cometh, that whosoever killeth
you will think that he doeth God service.[134]

Drug trafficking and use continue to grow to extremes of
practically having armies to defend these multibillion-dollar
industries against the legal armies of nations. More legaliza-
tion is sought and accomplished as societies blind themselves
to the consequences. Sexual deviancy is increasing with blatant
surges in homosexuality, pedophilia, bestiality, and violence.
No wonder God puts so much emphasis on the importance of
a sensitive conscience.

The subject of understanding and overcoming temptation
is of no interest to those who have dead consciences. They do
not have to be tempted to sin; sin is their life and their love.
A discussion of a dead conscience is included in this book to
simply complete the study of the scale of conscience. But more
important, it is to distinguish between the sins of those who fall
to temptation and those who willfully seek opportunity to sin.

---

134   John 16:2.

CHAPTER 7

Judgment of Those Who Fall to Temptation

The lack of distinction between the sins of those who fall to temptation and those who willfully seek opportunity to sin is one of the greatest injustices and hypocrisies in societies and in Christianity today. The two cases are very different and cannot and should not be judged in the same way. In the case of falling to temptation, we do not find a lack of proper values. This person may have strong spiritual values and a sincere sense of duty to struggle against the flesh and resist the temptation of the world and the Devil. As we have seen, however, this struggle is no easy matter, and even men like David, a *man after God's own heart,* are susceptible to falling. This is not evidence of a lack of a correct, sensitive conscience, but rather of the power of temptation.

Powers that Dominate the Will

The world recognizes many powers that dominate the will. Some of these powers are physical in nature. Certain substances are addictive, such as drugs and alcohol. The bodies of people who habitually use these substances become dependent to such a degree that their will cannot resist them but must seek them. Many programs and institutions have been developed to compassionately attempt rescue of these people from the bonds of addiction. Great amounts of money are spent by governments and private enterprises or groups for this cause. Laws are even made for their protection, and human rights groups are very involved. Doctors classify such addictions as sickness in order to take away the discomfort of recognizing it as sin and make it easier to accept that these people are dominated by this power.

Another power that dominates the will of man is pain. Much of the pain that he experiences is due to sickness. The anguish of some pain may so dominate the will as to drive him to despair, as in the case of Job. It may drive him to use drugs or occult practices in his desperate search for relief. Here again, society gives great attention to help these people find relief. The pain of hunger can drive people to go against normal values that direct the will and fall to thievery and even murder. Much pain is caused by other people. So great is the concern for these people that even wars are fought and lives given to achieve relief from such oppression.

Other powers that dominate the will are not physical but psychological or emotional. Nevertheless, they can dominate the will of man and cause him to do things he would normally not do. Actual pain is sometimes not necessary. The threat of pain and torture is enough to dominate the will of many. Emotional pain experienced when loved ones are lost through tragedies or divorce can cause irrational action of the will. Verbal abuse is recognized as having devastating effects on the proper development of the will in the lives of children, young people, and even adults. Deceit is used by wicked, devious people to incite emotions of hate and anger that also cause abnormal behavior.

In all of these cases of people falling into abnormal or even irrational behavior, much understanding and compassion exists in societies and in Christianity. For some reason, however, the power of temptation is not recognized. Yet, temptation is a power that dominates the will of man and destroys his ability to think and act in a way that will fulfill his right to well-being in life ("life, liberty and the pursuit of happiness"). It can damage a life as much as other powers condemned by society and should be treated the same as a harmful influence or substance.

Consider the following scale of domination of the will.

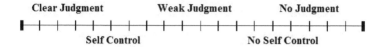

As a person comes under the influence of drugs or alcohol, for instance, their will goes from a point of clear judgment to weak judgment and, finally, to no judgment. This change in judgment represents the gradual loss of self-control, or in other words, the increasing domination of the will. Different degrees of pain, fears, loss, abuse, or deceit will also cause the weakening of judgment, a loss of self-control, and domination of the will.

Temptation

Temptation of man will have the same effect. This is a more universally dominating power than any of the others mentioned. No other power has caused as much abnormal behavior and damaging consequences. Yet there is little attention paid to this power in society today or, even in Christianity. Great efforts are made to warn the public and especially young people of the dangers of drugs. Even greater emphasis is placed on understanding how they work and what physical and psychological effects they will have on a human being. Other great efforts involve rehabilitation of drug users. However, little effort is made to understand the power of the temptation that actually causes the initial use of drugs or to educate people about this power. Even in Christianity, relatively few books have been written on the subject as compared to so many other subjects dealing with human experience.

Nancy Reagan's publicity program of "Just Say No" to drugs

indirectly recognized the power behind initial drug use but did not actually reveal the way the power works. Sometimes news stories appear of drug pushers using devious methods of temptation to seduce people to "just try" the drug. But other than mentioning the problem, little study or publicity occurs about how and why their methods work. Some effort is made to limit the temptation that advertisers of alcohol and tobacco can direct at young people, but no thorough explanation or education on the subject is given and the damage done to adults by these temptations is overlooked or excused as being their own, supposedly mature decision. This entire assumption ignores the power of temptation that dominates many people and causes them to make decisions against their better judgment.

Hypocrisy in Judgment

Worse than the lack of effort to understand and educate people about the power of temptation due to ignorance is the purposeful hiding of its significance in order to judge or slander someone who has fallen before its power, as if they were the same as others who willfully seek evil. If a person with high standards of moral right and wrong falls to the temptation to try alcohol or drugs, many people make no attempt to understand how the power of temptation induced him to act against the normal state of his will. Instead of making the effort to restore his self-control, he is judged and slandered as having a false morality and the same as others who have no standards at all. This applies to all areas of temptation.

One man succumbs to unwanted temptation of the natural appetites of the body while another actually desires the opportunity. One man forms a developed appetite due to the power of temptation over his will, while someone else forms these developed appetites without any resistance but actually fulfills what he wants. No greater hypocrisy is demonstrated today than the ignorant judgment of the two cases as being the same. Christianity as a whole is attacked by liberal, immoral groups with this tactic of ignoring and hiding the fact of the power of temptation and condemning those Christians who fall as if their faith is only a matter of convenience or influence. On the one hand, these people flaunt temptations of immorality, sensuality, and vice that take advantage of the natural appetites of the body and then condemn those who, in spite of a struggle, fall to this promoted temptation.

Liberal politicians are attempting to take this hypocrisy to the level of a planned strategy to destroy other men's reputations and lives for the sake of maintaining power that can be used to insure their own wicked gratification and greed. There is a great need to expose this hypocrisy and distinguish the difference between cases of falling to temptation and purposeful self-gratification.

Similar is the hypocrisy of condemning one unwanted temptation while promoting and flaunting another. Some will condemn drug use while defending the rights of those who tempt with pornography and education programs for supposed sexual awareness. Against all common human knowledge and experience, they promote an idea that unwanted moral temptation is simply a matter of preference, while other temptations such as drugs and alcohol are powers that excuse the behavior of those who fall in these areas.

This problem is not limited to immoral, liberal, and atheistic groups. It exists in Christianity also. Some people in churches and even some ministers are hypocrites living a double life. They have no true moral values and convictions but for one reason or another, merely make a show of being a Christian while actually willfully gratifying their personal desires. Others are true Christians with values and convictions of right and wrong that they respect and follow. However, these Christians and ministers struggle daily with the power of temptation and are susceptible to falling. Of course, sin is sin no matter who it is that commits it or what the character of that person is. Sin cannot be defended, and there will always be consequences. However, a vast difference exists between the two cases, and it is dishonest, improper, and unwise not to make the distinction when dealing with a person who has fallen.

For instance, if a church member is secretly and willfully living in adultery with no conscience of his sin, the Bible teaches that God plans to destroy such people, calling them *clouds [they are] without water, carried about of winds; trees whose fruit withereth, without fruit, twice dead, plucked up by the roots; Raging waves of the sea, foaming out their own shame; wandering stars, to whom is reserved the blackness of darkness for ever.*[135] The church is commanded *to deliver such an one unto Satan for the destruction of the flesh, that the spirit may be saved in the day of the Lord Jesus.*[136] If the church treats this kind of person as if he has simply fallen to temptation and as if the sin were against his values and convictions, the church will be secretly mocked by this person and others of the same two-faced character. Not only this, those who do have convictions and values will see an example of sin having little consequence, which can weaken their resistance to temptation.

The opposite situation occurs if a church member with clear values and convictions is seduced by the weakness of the flesh and falls to the temptation to commit adultery. The Bible teaches that this person should be rebuked for his sin[137] and restored by spiritual Christians in a spirit of meekness.[138] Even Jesus demonstrated this attitude with the woman taken in

---

135   Jude 1:12-13.
136   1 Corinthians 5:5.
137   1 Timothy 5:20.
138   Galatians 6:1.

adultery, saying *neither do I condemn thee: go, and sin no more.*[139] However, if this person is rejected and cast out of fellowship without an attempt to restore him, he may lose any hope of restoration and become hardened or despondent and never be restored. Besides this, some Christians may become vain in their own self-righteousness, which will weaken their resistance to temptation. Others struggling with the flesh may leave the fellowship of the church for fear of receiving the same treatment, since they know that they also are susceptible to falling.

Other circumstances and consequences are possible. Even the Corinthian man that Paul delivered to Satan apparently had his will broken by the consequences, humbled himself, and repented. After a change in character was demonstrated, the church was instructed *to forgive him, and comfort him, lest perhaps such a one should be swallowed up with overmuch sorrow.*[140] David's decision not to fully restore Absalom is another example of the importance of dealing honestly and justly with the motives of sin as well as with the sin itself.

Three Cases of Conflict

Sometimes this principle is demonstrated in dealing with a conflict between two people or groups of people. In any such conflict, three distinct cases are possible. First, the conflict may be between two who are both wrong in their attitudes and should both be rebuked and corrected. Second, both may be correct in their attitudes but cannot agree because of a difference in outlook, as in the case of the conflict between Paul and Barnabas.[141] In this case, neither can be judged nor rebuked but loved with patience and long-suffering until God reveals the correct solution. The third case has the greatest potential for

---

139 John 8:11.

140 2 Corinthians 2:7.

141 Acts 15:39 *And the contention was so sharp between them, that they departed asunder one from the other: and so Barnabas took Mark, and sailed unto Cyprus.*

incorrect judgment and spiritual damage. This is when one side of the conflict has the proper attitude and the other has a sinful attitude. If both are rebuked as being wrong without discerning the difference, the spiritual side will have been abused and may become disheartened, whereas the sinful side will have inadvertently been given more credibility by being treated as equal to the other. On the other hand, if both are treated as being spiritual like Paul and Barnabas, the truly spiritual side will suffer the abuse of being classified as the same as the sinful side and be mocked by that side. The sinful side will then be given an unjust and unmerited credibility that will only be used for more damage. In all of these examples, it becomes evident that understanding and overcoming temptation not only involves resistance to sin in one's own life, but also honest and righteous judgment[142] in the lives of others.

---

142 John 7:24.

Section 2

Overcoming Temptation

Before continuing with a description of the biblical steps to overcome temptation, you and I must agree on a foundation for any possible hope in the matter. That hope will only be found and experienced in accordance with our faith in what the Lord Jesus Christ can do through us by the power of the Holy Spirit. It is impossible to please God without faith that Christ is in us, and we are in Him. Without Him, we can do nothing. He is our life and our hope of being more than conquerors. However, although we know that it will be by His power alone that we can overcome temptation, our job is to walk in His steps. *It is He that worketh in you*, but it is you who by faith in Him must take up your cross and follow Him.

Jesus Christ's wisdom and power become a reality in our lives through the work of the Holy Spirit. The Holy Spirit produces that which magnifies Christ. He convicts of sin and teaches us the riches of the wisdom and understanding in Christ. When we walk in conformity to the ways and heart of our Savior, we know that the qualities of Christ that we demonstrate – love, joy, peace, longsuffering, gentleness, goodness, faith, meekness, temperance – are the result of the Holy Spirit's work.

The following steps are not a handbook to follow, but an aid for searching and yearning that will make clear the wisdom and power of Christ. Know that without Him any personal effort will be futile. Be comforted in knowing that He wants you to enjoy His overcoming power and the joy of victory over sin more than you do. In this quest to honor Christ, the Comforter is active in you with all sufficient power. You are not alone.

CHAPTER 8

God's Promise

A t the beginning of this book, we asked the questions, "Can we avoid this hurt and shame? Is there an answer that can actually be experienced? Can we enjoy the benefits of what is good, right, and wise, not only in our own life experiences but also in the lives of loved ones?" After attempting to thoroughly discuss the forces and factors involved in temptation, let us now return to these questions and provide true, practical answers. Analyzing and understanding all that is involved in the process of temptation is very difficult. Yet this is not as difficult as achieving the experience of overcoming temptation. In fact, after this study of the power of temptation and the experience of its continual effects upon our lives, we are tempted to laugh cynically and say "the conclusion is that it simply cannot be done."

Time after time, temptation has overcome us. Sometimes, we admit, there has been little resistance on our part. Other times guilt and shame have led us to determine to change our thoughts or actions that resulted from giving in to temptation. We had no lack of sincerity in truly desiring change. We even took some definite steps to avoid temptation or to resist it. This seemed to no avail, however, when after a short struggle, we were finally overcome once again. Each time this happened, our hope of overcoming seemed less and less possible.

The problem is that this experience is not in accord with how God assures us that we can overcome temptation. He dogmatically declares that *There hath no temptation taken you but such as is common to man: but God is faithful, who will not suffer you to be tempted above that ye are able; but will with the temptation also make a way to escape, that ye may be able to bear it.*[143]

Stanley refers to the point of this passage, saying: "Suffice it to say that *all* believers have the potential to say no to temptation, regardless of whether or not we are *perfect*. Pointing to character as an excuse for giving in to temptation holds no weight with God. We are all in the process of developing character, but where we are in that process has no bearing on our potential to overcome temptation. It may affect our *desire* to overcome temptation, but not our *ability*."[144]

If victory over temptation is really possible, then something must be wrong with the way we have faced or resisted temptation so far. The question is, then, not how many times we have failed, but why have we failed? What has been our ineffective way of resisting and what is the effective way that God teaches and provides?

---

143 1 Corinthians 10:13.
144 Stanley, *Winning the War Within*, 17.

CHAPTER 9

Preparation of the Heart

Another question arises here. How sincerely do I want to overcome temptation? How deep is my desire to experience victory?

Owen says, "Do not allow your heart to be content with the status quo for one moment. In the natural and material realm, longing desires are useless unless they are reinforced by a diligent exercise to fulfill them. But with spiritual things it is otherwise. Longing, breathing, and panting after deliverance is a grace in itself, having a mighty power to conform the soul to the likeness of the thing longed after. The apostle, describing the repentance and godly sorrow of the Corinthians, speaks of this as "vehement desire" (2 Corinthians 7:11). In the context of speaking about indwelling sin in Romans 7, he breaks out in longing desire to be rid of it. Unless we long for deliverance we will never have it."[145]

This "longing" for deliverance can be felt by someone who has struggled with temptation in the past and knows that it will come again. Or it can be felt when one is in the middle of temptation when longing for peace is obscured by the flesh's fear of losing its source of gratification.

Owen mentions this probable difficulty in David's temptation, saying: "On the other hand, David remained allured by his present enjoyment with Bathsheba, for whom he lusted. Sin sometimes carries men away by their love for sin, and they continue in it because they fear what will ensue if they stop."[146]

145 Owen, *Sin and Temptation*, 177.
146 Owen, *Sin and Temptation*, 107.

If the mind is occupied with this fear of losing something, the longing for deliverance will be weakened. Knowing this, if one longs for deliverance, he needs to focus on the longing. He should visualize victory and fill his mind and emotions with the peace and benefits of victory that the longing will increase and occupy the mind more and more.

When the desire to overcome temptation is strong, one should consciously prepare for the battle against temptation beforehand. The fact is that if you do not "plan to stand," you are actually "planning to fall." Preparation for temptation is essential. Doing nothing to prevent temptation is how one "plans to fall."

Stanley says, "A general whose task is to defend a city against attack doesn't wait until the city is being besieged to plan his defense. A wise general plans his defense strategy long before the threat of attack even presents itself. 'How will the enemy attack? From which direction will they approach? Where are our weak spots?' These are some of the questions a general should ask when preparing his defenses. Likewise believers should sit down ahead of time and plan their defense against temptation."[147]

This indispensable preparation involves our attitudes and heart. On the positive side, we must fill our heart with love for God. The more personally and intimately we know him and commune with him, the more temptation's offers will be abhorred.

Owen expresses this need, saying: "We need to keep our heart full of a sense of the love of God. This is the greatest preservative available to us against the power of temptation in the world. Joseph demonstrates this by crying, 'How then can I do this great evil, and sin against God?' (Genesis 39:9). Temptation could not hold him, but left him alone. When the

---

147 Stanley, *Winning the War Within*, 75.

love of Christ constrains us to live for him, then we can with-stand temptation."[148]

On the negative side, we must be serious about sin every day. The danger must not be forgotten or underestimated. We should look at "small" sins as filthy flies that should be shooed away knowing the serious contamination they can cause.

Again Owen says, "The most saintly believers, who appear free from the condemning power of sin, make it their duty every day to mortify the indwelling power of sin. Paul exhorts us in Colossians 3:5, 'Mortify therefore your members which are upon the earth.' He is, saying: 'Make it your daily occupation. Do not cease a day from this work. Be killing sin or it will kill you.' Jesus tells us the Father constantly prunes every living branch of the vine, so that it will bear more fruit (John 15:2)."[149]

Since we know that temptation is a battle for the will, we must keep our will humble by consciously acknowledging the total weakness of our flesh and its unworthiness of any merit apart from its submission to the Lord's will and service. The sinful fruit of its influence should be feared.

"Indeed, the fear of sin and the fear of the Lord are the same thing" says Owen.[150] The problem with humility is that it must be complete and universal or it will be corrupted. This makes it very fragile. In fact, one of Satan's most common attacks against humility is to give thoughts of satisfaction with one's humility that can easily make one "proud of being humble."

Screwtape instructs his demon nephew to: "Catch him at the moment when he is really poor in spirit and smuggle into his mind the gratifying reflection, 'By Jove! I'm being humble,' and almost immediately pride – pride at his own humility – will appear."[151]

---

148 Owen, *Sin and Temptation*, 132.
149 Owen, *Sin and Temptation*, 160.
150 Owen, *Sin and Temptation*, 40.
151 Lewis, *Screwtape Letters*, 71.

Besides this subtle attack with pride, humility will be corrupted with any other harbored sin. Making the mistake of tolerating some sin is easy because of how much other sins are hated. We are considering ourselves "pretty humble," or in other words we are willing to submit in many areas, but there is some "small" area in which we are not willing to submit. Unfortunately, this acceptance of being "pretty humble" really means that our will reserves the final decision about how much to submit, and this attitude is not true humility at all. True humility is recognizing the superiority of God's ways in all things and his sovereign right to rule what is his, which produces in us a willingness and desire to submit to him in all areas of life.

Owen rightly explains, "Without obedience to all of God's Word and all of God's provisions for salvation, isolated acts of mortification avail little. Universal obedience is essential. The apostle urges us, 'Cleanse ourselves from all filthiness of the flesh and spirit, perfecting holiness in the fear of God' (2 Cor. 7:1). Hating one particular sin or weakness is not enough; we must have a general disposition of life before God. The outbreak of one particular sin may only be symptomatic of the general condition of sickness, for sin lies at the root of our being. Thus God allows one sin to perplex us and gain strength over us, in order to chasten us and allow us to see lukewarmness before the Lord."[152]

Nothing is more important to prepare our hearts beforehand for the battle with temptation than this attitude of humility or universal obedience. The tendency of our heart is to think we can just control temptation instead of seeing the need to eliminate it.

Jerry and Kirsti Newcombe point out this subtle danger, saying: "Part of what makes resisting temptation so hard is that we want to dabble with it. But that's sort of like gently flirting

152   Owen, *Sin and Temptation,* 166.

with another man's wife. Franklin P. Jones said, 'What makes resisting temptation difficult, for many people, is that they don't want to discourage it completely.' That is so true. But if you play with fire, you can expect to get burned. Josh Billings pointed out, 'One-half of the trouble of this life can be traced to saying yes too quick, and not saying no soon enough.' If we could become more like Joseph in that we don't even entertain the possibility and we diligently flee the scene when temptation rears its ugly head, we'd go a long way in resisting temptation when it comes knocking."[153]

This is one of Satan's traps that he uses to maintain breaches in our defense plan. Part of our preparation against temptation is to understand that one sin leads to another.

Stanley explains, "Along the same lines, a third reason you must once again take up the battle against the sinful elements of your lifestyle is that one sin always leads to another. Sin is like a cancer in that it spreads. One undealt-with area opens up other areas as well. Once you become accustomed to a particular sin, once it becomes entrenched in your lifestyle, it is only a matter of time until other areas become problems. It seems like most of the counseling sessions I am involved in begin with a story about some small sin that was allowed to go undealt with. This one area opened the door for other things that soon blossomed into major problems."[154]

If we truly want to overcome temptation and experience the peace and abundant benefits of God's will in our lives, families, and relationships, we must face this decision of being humble before God. All the factors of how to overcome temptation that will be studied in this book are founded on this disposition of our heart. Too often we are instead trying to justify and protect certain activities or relationships as not being wrong, instead

---

153   Newcombe, *A Way of Escape,* 210.
154   Stanley, *Winning the War Within,* 13-14.

of humbly considering what is God's will and being willing to follow him.

Stanley says, "When we are faced with decisions about opportunities, invitations, vacations, gifts, movies, music, books, magazines, videos, dates, or anything else that pertains to our daily lives, we shouldn't be asking, 'What's wrong with this?' Instead we should be asking, What is the wise thing to do?'"[155]

He then mentions the exhortation in Ephesians 5:15, *See then that ye walk circumspectly, not as fools, but as wise* and he concludes, "We must get in the habit of testing each opportunity in light of our past experience, present weaknesses, and future plans. My experience as a pastor tells me that people rarely plan to get into trouble. Their problem is that they fail to plan to stay out of trouble."[156]

This is a very practical application of the necessary attitude of humility. Later Stanley refers to Ephesians 5:17, *Wherefore be ye not unwise, but understanding what the will of the Lord is* and forcefully exhorts, "What Paul means is this: 'Don't go on willfully ignoring what you know in your heart God would have you to do. Face up to it!' Paul is calling us to quit playing games; to quit excusing those things in our lives that may not be "wrong" but lead us into sin time and time again. 'Quit rationalizing away those relationships that keep causing you to stumble. Only a fool continues to play games with himself!' he admonishes."[157]

---

155 Stanley, *Winning the War Within*, 103.
156 Stanley, *Winning the War Within*, 104.
157 Stanley, *Winning the War Within*, 110.

CHAPTER 10

Useless Methods

Before studying God's ways, we must look at some of the common ways man faces temptation that are not only not taught by God but are, on the contrary, said to be hopeless. First, it is common to indulge in wishful thinking about not having desires or temptations. We wish we simply did not have the emotional reactions to circumstances or the passions that overpower our wills. We wonder how nice it would be if there were some way of simply turning these reactions and feelings off, the same as we turn off the lights with a switch. We pray that God would take the temptation away or make us different and unconsciously imply through this that it is somewhat God's fault. We even get angry with God sometimes for his supposed lack of intervention. This wishful thinking, however, is an illusion. God does not promise us that there will be no temptation. He promises us a way of escape. He does not promise to make us different so we will not feel tempted. He promises that there is victory if we will learn and follow this way of escape. There is nothing useful or wise in this wishful thinking, and it only serves to cause discouragement and distract us from what we ought to be thinking about and doing. These illusions are another temptation in themselves and certainly not a solution.

More common is the sense of struggling against temptation as a matter of duty. This is very confusing and somewhat disheartening, because no one doubts the matter of our duty to do right. However, we find that this struggle against temptation as dutiful becomes a wearisome task that may seem to work for a while but finally ends in failure. The length of the struggle may vary according to the strength of a person's will and the personal discipline that has been developed, but lasting victory is not achieved. The problem is not that there is something wrong with a sense of duty: The problem has to do with the focus of our mind and heart.

To shed some light on this situation consider the following Scriptures. To the Colossians Paul writes, *Wherefore if ye be dead with Christ from the rudiments of the world, why, as though living in the world, are ye subject to ordinances, (Touch not; taste not; handle not; which all are to perish with the using;) after the commandments and doctrines of men? Which things have indeed a shew of wisdom in will worship, and humility, and neglecting of the body; not in any honour to the satisfying of the flesh. If ye then be risen with Christ, seek those things which are above, where Christ sitteth on the right hand of God. Set your affection on things above, not on things on the earth.*[158] To the Corinthians he declares, *The sting of death is sin; and the strength of sin is the law.*[159]

Here we can see that there is a way in which a struggle to fulfill right as a matter of duty will fail. If this struggle is only according to law, there will be weakness, and that will result in finally being overcome. This was the point in Paul's teachings to the Jews – that their righteousness according to the law was vain and their only hope was the righteousness according to the gospel of Christ.[160] Under the law, man found himself condemned. Only under grace did he find salvation. Under the law, the struggle to do right is carried on in man's own human strength which fails to overcome the appetites of the flesh. Even when we are saved by grace, if we again resort to this human

---

158 Colossians 2:20-3:2.
159 1 Corinthians 15:56.
160 Romans 3:19-26.

strength as our way of resisting temptation, we will experience weakness and eventual failure.

In the Scriptures, God presents three inseparable and essential factors for overcoming temptation. These three factors are the knowledge of the truth, the power of the Holy Spirit, and faith. The challenge is to know the truth, to understand the power of the Holy Spirit, and to access this power by faith through believing the truth and trusting in the Holy Spirit. It is not entirely possible to study these factors in any correct order because they are so interrelated. The Word reveals to us the person and work of the Holy Spirit, yet the Holy Spirit reveals to us the meaning of the Word.[161] We trust in the Spirit by faith and yet faith is a fruit of the Spirit.[162] This must be kept in mind as we study these three factors.

---

161 1 Corinthians 2:14.
162 Galatians 5:22.

CHAPTER 11

Truth

Jesus related victory to truth, saying: *And ye shall know the truth, and the truth shall make you free.*[163] In the broadest sense, truth is the whole mind of God. What is knowledge to him is truth to us. More specifically, truth is that part of the mind of God that is revealed to us in the Scriptures, God's Word. Jesus spoke of this factor in overcoming temptation when he prayed, saying: *Sanctify them through thy truth. Thy Word is truth.*[164] This makes it very clear how important the Word is to overcoming temptation. If there is a lack of knowledge of the Scriptures, one will be much more susceptible to temptation. If there is a lack of trust in the Scriptures, one will have no hope of overcoming temptation.

Here we see the two relationships that man has to the Scriptures. First, he must know them and second, he must trust them. The first relationship determines the amount of truth that is known. When we read or hear that God says he *will make a way* to escape any temptation, our minds are exposed to truth. We are no longer ignorant of this promise, and in this we have taken a great step forward. However, this knowledge of the truth is of little value if we do not sincerely believe it. It is not just *knowing* that God said he *will make a way* but actually *believing* that he *will make a way* which will produce a desire and determination to obey God's will and escape temptation. Someone said, "If you say you can or you can't, you're right." This saying

---

163   John 8:32.
164   John 17:17.

can be applied very well to the principle of needing to not only know the Scriptures but sincerely trust them. If you do trust them and therefore believe you can overcome, you will be on the road to achieving that victory. If you doubt the Scriptures and therefore do not believe you can overcome, you will have little motivation or spiritual power to apply the Scriptures to your life, which will result in weakness when facing temptation. These principles make it clear that overcoming temptation will depend upon the amount of time we spend reading, studying, and meditating upon God's Word, and also upon our attitude of trusting or not trusting what we learn from God.

Truth and the Conscience

To reinforce these two principles, we need to analyze how this works. Earlier, we discussed the importance of our conscience and how God uses it as a sensor to detect right and wrong. We learned that the conscience depends upon the correct source of knowledge of truth in order to correctly guide us. If some of our knowledge is based on error, our conscience may give us a sense of doing right when we are doing wrong. This emphasizes the need to determine the truth as God reveals it in his Word and to reject any knowledge that is not in accord with that truth.

The conscience is a critical part of overcoming temptation. To have the benefit of this sensor we must both supply it with a foundation of true knowledge of what is right and what is wrong and protect its sensitivity by not violating its direction. Not trusting the Word will produce this violation of the conscience, which will result in its dullness and, as a consequence, in a loss of protection from temptation. If this is understood, we will avoid reasoning and excuses that seem harmless but are actually damaging to the conscience. Even humor can be used by Satan to damage the conscience.

Screwtape affirms, "Humor is for them the all-consoling

and (mark this) the all-excusing, grace of life. Hence it is invaluable as a means of destroying shame. If a man simply lets others pay for him, he is 'mean'; if he boasts of it in a jocular manner and twits his fellows with having been scored off, he is no longer 'mean' but a comical fellow. Mere cowardice is shameful; cowardice boasted of with humorous exaggerations and grotesque gestures can be passed off as funny. Cruelty is shameful—unless the cruel man can represent it as a practical joke. A thousand bawdy, or even blasphemous, jokes do not help towards a man's damnation so much as the discovery that almost anything he wants to do can be done, not only without the disapproval but with the admiration of his fellows, if only it can get itself treated as a Joke."[165]

The conscience must be considered a primary defense against temptation. Jesus said, *Watch and pray that ye enter not into temptation.*[166] Part of this watchfulness depends upon the state of the conscience. If the conscience is built on truth and its sensitivity is maintained, we will be much more able to watch and pray and experience victory over temptation.

If the conscience has already been violated to the point that it gives little protection, it is essential to "tune it back up." This is not a simple or quick process, but it can be done. First, sin must be confessed. Repentance and conviction of sin will not be deeply felt when the conscience is dull. However, the mind is still capable of knowing the truth and agreeing with God as far as right and wrong are concerned. This agreement with God is the essence of confession of sin and will help the conscience to become more sensitive again. Prayer is another part of the process. If one is sincere in asking God to restore his conscience, God will use both the attitude of our heart in

---

165 Lewis, *Screwtape Letters,* 59.
166 Matthew 26:41.

recognizing the value of the conscience and his own plan to bring about that restoration.

Owen suggests, "Persuade your conscience to listen diligently to all that the law says about your lust and corruption. If you will ever mortify your sins, it must be as your conscience arms itself with a clear and thorough apprehension of the law. Like David, let your iniquity be ever before you (Psalm 51:3)."[167]

Since the conscience depends so much on knowledge, one must spend definite time meditating on principles of right and wrong, evil and good, the works of God and the tactics of Satan. As the mind is filled with the value of good and the ugliness and damage of evil, the conscience will begin to regain sensitivity.

Recognizing the development of the conscience in children is of grave importance. Although a child's conscience may not have been dulled by violations, the child is still developing. Sometimes parents simply excuse disobedience, disrespect, or rebellion in their children, calling it childishness that will somehow change to maturity. By doing this, they will stunt the development of the child's conscience, leaving the door open for it to be seared at an early age with long-range consequences. Correct training and discipline are indispensable when fostering in children the knowledge base and sensitivity to protect them from the dangers and consequences of temptation.

Since the feelings of guilt and shame are products of the conscience that are lost when it is dulled or seared, a more drastic action may be necessary to re-stimulate these emotions. Public confession of sin is one example of such an act, but it is uncommon. Such confession does maintain the potential of causing shame that will motivate us to abstain from sin. Once this shame is experienced, the mind again relates the sin to shame, and the emotion is reawakened by the conscience.

Some instances of public confession are limited and simple

---

167   Owen, *Sin and Temptation*, 175.

but nevertheless very powerful in developing the conscience. If parents find that a child has stolen something, they may discipline him, which will help the sensitivity of the conscience. However, if the child is made to return the stolen item and to confess his sin to the affected party, an even greater shame results, and the conscience will be more sensitive to the wrong.

Other instances are more far-reaching. Public confession before the church can serve to reinforce the conscience to recognize sin and resist temptation. A person should be instructed as to the purpose of such public confession so its effect will be proper and not just a punishment or humiliation. The consciences of the other church members will also be strengthened by the example alone. Paul rebuked Peter publicly on one occasion[168] and James also instructed the church to practice public confession.[169] The last step of Jesus' teaching on church discipline and reconciliation also involves this principle.[170]

Accountability is another principle involved in developing and tuning up a dulled conscience. This involves being held accountable for one's actions, words, or attitudes by another person who will help to set a high standard of character and integrity. For instance, a person could establish a relationship with a pastor, parent, or Christian friend, for the specific purpose of being answerable for behavior over a period of time.

Stanley describes this effective method, saying: "Specifically, what we are talking about here is a relationship with a person or a small group of people in which you can share anything: your hurts, your fears, your temptations, your victories, and even your defeats. It must be a relationship committed to honesty, openness and, above all, privacy."[171]

Many churches are using accountability groups. Groups of

---

168   Galatians 2:11.
169   James 5:16.
170   Matthew 18:15-17.
171   Stanley, *Winning the War Within,* 147.

men or women meet together weekly or monthly to hold one another accountable. All participants know they will be asked personal questions about their behavior and will have to respond publicly. This serves to develop the correct ability to feel shame and guilt and results in a greater resistance to temptation as they avoid situations that can cause these uncomfortable feelings.

Another way to use accountability for a positive purpose is to publicly teach or write about truths of right and wrong. When a person teaches or writes on these subjects, he will feel a great sense of being held accountable by his listeners or readers to practice what he preaches or live up to what he writes. Can you imagine the pressure on the apostle Paul to show a continual attitude and practice of divine love towards others after writing 1 Corinthians 13? Believe me, it is with "fear and trembling" that I write on this subject of temptation, and it brings to mind the fear Paul expressed when he said, *But I keep under my body, and bring it into subjection: lest that by any means, when I have preached to others, I myself should be a castaway.*[172]

The reason a person might want to become involved in accountability to another person or group or by teaching or writing is that the consequences of falling to temptation are more disastrous. The practicing of accountability that develops sensitivity of the conscience and prevents falling to temptation is much to be preferred.

Stanley says, "So you are left with a choice to make. Are you willing to expose your weaknesses to a hand-picked individual or group now, or would you rather run the risk of having your weaknesses exposed to the whole world later? We all need somebody to talk to. Don't let your pride keep you from finding somebody. The more prominent and successful you become, the more you need accountability. Unfortunately, it will become increasingly difficult to find because people may

---

172   1 Corinthians 9:27.

be intimidated. 'Who am I to offer him advice?' they may ask. But don't give up. There may come a time in your life when your accountability partner is all that stands between you and disaster."[173]

We understand that the conscience loses sensitivity gradually by an almost unnoticeable, progressive increase in activities that start out as innocent and eventually lead to that which is questionable and finally, to outright sinfulness.

Screwtape reveals this tactic, saying: "We know that we have introduced a change of direction in his course which is already carrying him out of his orbit around the Enemy; but he must be made to imagine that all the choices which have effected this change of course are trivial and revocable. He must not be allowed to suspect that he is now, however slowly, heading right away from the sun on a line which will carry him into the cold and dark of utmost space."[174]

Undoing this process, therefore, involves pushing our activities back the other way so as to regain sensitivity. The first step is to eliminate that which is sinful and the questionable activities. However, due to the loss of sensitivity and the need to restore it, it is often necessary to go even further the other way by limiting freedoms that were once considered innocent but might be the gradual loss of sensitivity. This can involve limitations or changes in relationships, entertainment, education, jobs, or even churches. We see then, that the conscience can be developed or "tuned up," so our knowledge and acceptance of truth as a factor in overcoming temptation will be enhanced.

Truth and Christ

We must understand that besides having the truth revealed to us through the written Word of God, we also have the truth

---

173 Stanley, *Winning the War Within,* 155.
174 Lewis, *Screwtape Letters,* 61.

through the testimony of the life and character of Christ Jesus and through his example of resisting temptation. All truth has purpose, and the purpose is related to the character of Christ. Truth that is separated from the character of Christ loses its purpose and is no longer used correctly. Many sins are committed as a result of a staunch loyalty to truth but without imitating the character of our model, the Lord Jesus Christ. The truth that is used our way, not God's way, will become a **part** of temptation and not a part of **overcoming** temptation.

Christ is not only the living example of the correct use and purpose of truth, but also the practical example of resisting temptation. One of his many purposes in becoming man was to identify with us and demonstrate to us that he understands our struggles. His understanding gives us great comfort and hope. This understanding was especially related to our experience of temptation because he *was in all points tempted like as we are, yet without sin.*[175] The fact that he could not sin in no way diminishes this ability to understand and, as a result, his desire to help us in temptation.[176]

One of the ways he helps us is by his example of resisting Satan's temptation. Matthew 4:1-11 and Luke 4:1-13 record this example. This truth not only dispels the subtle lies that Satan attempts to make others believe, but also dispels the lie about his power over us. Satan tried, as always, to tempt Jesus in the three basic areas of man's weakness: *the lust of the flesh, the lust of the eyes and the pride of life.*[177] These three areas of weakness also correspond to the three enemies of man – the flesh, the world, and Satan. The way Jesus dealt with each area of temptation, revealed both by the written Word and the character of Christ, is the example that we must follow.

---

175   Hebrews 4:15.
176   Hebrews 2:18.
177   1 John 2:16.

Understanding an Attack

According to the order of events found both in Matthew 4 and Luke 4, Jesus was first tempted in the area of the lust of the flesh.

> *And when he had fasted forty days and forty nights, he was afterward an hungred. And when the tempter came to him, he said, If thou be the Son of God, command that these stones be made bread. But he answered and said, It is written, Man shall not live by bread alone, but by every word that proceedeth out of the mouth of God.*

This is an example of temptation in just one of the weaknesses of the flesh, but it establishes truths and patterns to follow in order for the believer to overcome temptation in all weaknesses. First, Jesus knew what was happening. In spite of his hunger, he was not taken off guard. Our first defense, then, is to thoroughly understand the weakness of the flesh, so we will not be taken by surprise when temptation comes.

Owen admonishes that, "We need to know our own heart, our natural disposition, and the lusts, corruptions, and spiritual weaknesses that beset us. Our Savior told the disciples, 'Ye know not what manner of spirit ye are of' (Luke 9:55). They had ambition and the desire for revenge. Had they known it they would have watched themselves. David tells us he considered his ways and kept himself from the iniquity to which he was prone (Psalm 18:23)."[178]

We have seen that one of the most important points in understanding temptation was to see the flesh as being weak from God's viewpoint (see page 14), and not as being strong from man's viewpoint. This sets our mind in the correct attitude to face this temptation.

Second, Jesus understood the consequences of his actions.

---

178   Owen, *Sin and Temptation*, 130.

He knew that the satisfaction of his appetite of hunger was not at all the point of Satan's temptation. Satan desired his will in any way possible so God would not be honored and his plan would not be fulfilled. Jesus saw his trap clearly. As Psalm 119:110 says, *The wicked have laid a snare for me: yet I erred not from thy precepts.* He had come to be the perfect sacrifice offered for man's sin. If he satisfied even a legitimate need of food in his own way according to his own will, he would not be in submission to his Father's will, and that is the essence of sin. His purpose would fail and man would be lost. This is in contrast with Eve, who fell for Satan's lie and false authoritative declaration. She did not see beyond the fruit to the grave consequences that would affect the rest of her life, the lives of her entire family and of all mankind. Had she seen the consequences clearly, the temptation would not have been attractive at all.

In describing how Satan obscures the consequences of sin Owen says, "Third, it *hides the danger* associated with sin. Sin covers the hook with bait, and spreads the food over the net. It is, of course, impossible for sin to completely remove the knowledge of danger from the soul. It cannot remove the reality that 'the wages of sin is death (Romans 6:23), or hide 'the judgment of God, that they who commit sin are worthy of death' (Romans 1:32). But it so takes up and possesses the mind and affections with the attraction and desirability of sin, that it diverts the soul from realizing its danger."[179]

Knowing Satan's expertise in obscuring the consequences of actions, we must be aware of the deceit of delights that do not appear to have serious consequences, such as social drinking, lotteries, so-called "soft" pornography, and so on.

Nehemiah, on the other hand, did not fall for Satan's lies. When he was "cordially" invited to a meeting by some of the men of the country for the "noble" purpose of "eliminating

---

179 Owen, *Sin and Temptation*, 61.

misunderstandings and working out their differences," Nehemiah saw their true motives and intentions. Later, these men sent word about a "rumor" that might damage his relation to the king, insinuating that if he did not meet with them to "discuss" the rumor, he might have problems. Again Nehemiah was not deceived and understood their true intentions. After this, a man from his own city seemed concerned about his safety and told him that he was going to be attacked and he should hide in the temple. In all of these traps of deceit, Nehemiah perceived the truth and did not fall. On the contrary, he experienced a great victory.[180]

Perceiving the truth is one of our greatest needs to overcome temptation. We must maximize the consequences and minimize the benefits. This principle alone may have made all the difference when David, Solomon, Samson, and others were tempted. It will make a great difference in our experience. To do this, we must fill our minds with stories in the Bible about terrible consequences that were suffered when people fell to temptation. Scriptures such as Proverbs 6:27, *Can a man take fire into his bosom, and his clothes not be burned?* open our eyes to look beyond the temptation to the consequences. The passages in Proverbs 9:13-18 and 7:6-23 paint a picture for us of the simple-minded ignorance of one who is tempted and does not see the consequences that will follow. The apostle Paul warned the Thessalonians that his labor would be in vain if they succumbed to temptation.[181] The more truth we have about temptation and its consequences, the greater clarity our minds will have in its face, and the stronger our resistance will be.

This knowledge will also be reinforced by meditating on people's experiences in Scripture and even of those living around us. Some of these examples will be of the consequences of

---

180   Nehemiah 6:1-14.
181   1 Thessalonians 3:5.

falling to temptation and others will be of the results of resisting temptation. Both the negative and the positive are necessary to give our minds the ability to see beyond the temptation to the consequences. Every detail that David suffered as a result of his fall should stick in our minds. We should see that by sowing to the flesh he set himself up to fall to greater sins of murder and deceit. His good reputation that cost years of sacrifice and faithfulness was destroyed. His daughter was raped by his own son, Amnon. Another son, Absalom, murdered Amnon and forced David himself to flee for his life. Absalom also died violently, causing even deeper sorrow in David's life. The consequences go on and on. Each example highlights the deceit of temptation. On the other hand, we have examples such as Joseph, who resisted and rejected temptation. In Joseph's life, we see the great benefits that came because of his faithfulness but also all that could have been lost had he given in to temptation.

At the same time we maximize the consequences of temptation in our minds, we also must minimize the temporal benefits. As the flesh demands satisfaction of each of its appetites and offers gratifying sensations, we should see how short-lived that satisfaction and sensation really are. Even though the God-given sensations can be justly experienced in the proper way, the sensations are momentary. They have little effect on our general prosperity and well-being and soon leave us with the same emptiness and desire. They are not worth the grave, long-range consequences that come when they are fulfilled sinfully. When they are fulfilled justly, we can enjoy the gratifying sensations with a clear conscience, no fear of consequences, and the experience of the tremendous superiority of righteousness.

The second temptation of Jesus in Luke 4 had to do with the *lust of the eyes* and corresponds to our second enemy, the world. Satan knew that Jesus was interested in people. He attempted to dangle that interest before him and make it seem possible to have what he wanted. The great goal was made to appear achievable. Satan, as usual, seemed concerned for his well-being and willing to cooperate if Jesus would do his part. The part required of Jesus did not seem so difficult; he merely had to ignore his conscience, complete a simple act, and receive the great reward that was offered.

This great reward did not attract Jesus for a second because, once again, he knew the truth. As in the first temptation, he saw the deceit of Satan and the consequences that would follow. This truth exposed Satan as a liar. Jesus' desire to save the world could not be fulfilled Satan's way. God's way is the only way.

As in the first temptation, this sets an example for us to follow. Jesus not only knew the truth, he is the truth. As we fill our minds with the wisdom of his Word and with his person, we too will detect the lies of Satan when he offers us the things of the world. When the *cares of the world* catch our attention and tempt us to worry about how to have what we need for our well-being, comfort, or acceptance, the truth of the Word and the person of Christ is what will eliminate those cares. His promises show us the way to true security, comfort, and acceptance, while the true end of Satan's way is revealed as causing loss, heartache, and shame. When riches are presented as being desirable and as our source of joy, power, security, and achievement, the truth of the Word and the person of Christ will reveal the deceit of the world's riches. We will see how insecure they are and the emptiness they actually bring.

Justifying Error

Finally, Satan attempted to use the *pride of life* to influence Jesus' actions. He had failed to get Jesus to go against the Word of truth, so he presented this temptation as if it were a fulfillment of that Word. He quoted the Word and made it easy to reason that the reputation of the truth of the Word was at stake.

Again, Satan knows what the greatest interest of each person is and knows how to use that interest in his temptation. In Jesus' case, he used the Lord's love and zeal for the Word as a motivation to act. If he did act, it would seem to justify the Word. If he did not, it would seem to cast doubt on the truth of the Word. With us Satan will know just how to tempt us according to our interests. Parents will be led to prove their love for their children by abstaining from discipline, defending their child's behavior or putting their studies above all else. Preachers may feel a need to justify a particular stand on a religious issue by cutting off fellowship with other pastors, dropping support of missionaries, or trying to influence members of other churches through newsletters or mass media. Doctors will feel a need to justify their concern for people's health, lawyers for people's rights, and politicians for people's fair treatment. Something will always need to be shown as being right when, in truth, Satan is trying to get people to act according to their own will and not the will of God.

The truth prevailed once again, however, because Jesus knew that it was not the reputation of the Word that was at stake at all, but rather his submission to the Father's will. He saw through the pressure that was applied to the hidden motives and purposes of Satan and so felt no need to justify the Word in that way. On the contrary, in each of these three temptations, he used the Word rightly, according to its designed purpose, to reject and defeat Satan's temptation.

Satan himself is the third enemy and the master of the other two. It is he who incites the flesh and entices the world. He is the antithesis of truth, the father of lies.[182] Any desire to overcome temptation must include resisting the Devil. We have seen that Satan's work is mostly through the mind. He attempts to sow evil thoughts without a person knowing that he is the origin

---

182 John 8:44.

of the thoughts and not the person himself. In this way, he can torment and tempt until patterns of thinking and attitudes are formed, making his work all the easier. He cannot work if there is truth that destroys his lies and reveals his activity. Our first need then is both to know the truth in all areas of right and wrong and also to know the truth about Satan himself – his evil nature and methods of working.

Although Owen focuses on indwelling sin, it is evident that he is also describing this need to know Satan's tactics when he says, "Second, it is important to learn the wiles and tactics of sin before engaging in spiritual warfare. This is what men do in dealing with their enemies. They gather intelligence about the designs and strategies of the enemy. Without such spying and intelligence work, war would be reduced to a brutish affair. It is the same with sin. Observe the ways of evil, and then prevent them. David learned, 'My sin is ever before me (Psalm 51:3). It is important to learn the subtleties, policies, and depth of indwelling sin. Learn to recognize its typical excuses, pleas and pretenses. Then in anticipation of its wiles stay on guard."[183]

Knowledge of the Word

Knowing the truth of right and wrong with a good conscience will cause us to react to his lies and know they are wrong. Knowing the truth about Satan will reveal in a particular moment that it is he who is attacking us by subtly sowing the lies. Knowing the truth about right and wrong involves a thorough knowledge of the Word of God and an attitude of agreeing with God about those truths. Knowing the truth about Satan involves a thorough knowledge of the teachings of the Word about him and an attitude of watchfulness to catch him in the act of sowing thoughts in the mind.[184]

183 Owen, *Sin and Temptation*, 157-158.
184 Read *Why You Really Can Memorize Scripture*, by Dr. Daniel Morris, for more on the power of scripture memorization.

If a person desires to overcome temptation, one easy and practical step is to determine a plan of daily reading and studying a portion of the Word of God. As one studies, he must look for truth, not only by reading what God says, but also by understanding why he said it. The Word will clarify itself in most cases, and the Holy Spirit will be involved in the clarification. God also sends preachers and teachers of the Word to clarify these truths. Memorization of large passages is a little more work but brings great advances in understanding the purposes of God's Word.

Stanley says, "There are no good excuses. It really comes down to one thing: Laziness. We are just too lazy to fill the arsenal of our minds with those truths we need to combat the lies of the enemy. And consequently, when he attacks, we get wiped out."[185]

Memorization should not be based on a set amount of Scriptures each day, but rather on a set amount of time. This will eliminate the pressure that is counterproductive and simply allow the memory to work the way God created it to work.

Satan will not be idle during this time of study; he will either seek to inhibit the study or to distort the knowledge and understanding. He will attempt to make a person form conclusions beforehand and then study to prove the conclusions, instead of studying to learn God's truth. He has already deceived many, so there will be an abundance of literature and messages of *false teachers*.[186] Because of this, a person must do more than increase his knowledge of the truth of right and wrong. He must also increase his knowledge of the truth about Satan and the need for watchfulness to detect him sowing thoughts in the mind, either directly or by way of teachers whom he has deceived.

As mentioned before, Satan uses devices to control the mind.

---

185   Stanley, *Sin and Temptation*, 136.
186   2 Peter 2:1; Matthew 24:11; Acts 20:30.

His tools such as TV, music, and literature have been considered, as well as his use of influences of sinful people. His subtle use of weaknesses that have to do with particular circumstances or age (page 26) have been observed as well as his method of avoiding detection and resistance by producing gradual change (page 28). How he subtly causes error by getting Christians to focus on one or the other of the inseparable qualities of faith and obedience has also been studied.

Watchfulness

When ignorance of truth is not the problem, what remains is the more difficult task of forming the habit of watchfulness and actually resisting him. Owen emphasizes the grave importance of habitually being watchful by looking at the failures of some of the Bible's great men:

"It is significant that these men received great and wonderful mercies from the hand of God before sin invaded their lives, but they failed to remain diligent and watchful. God delivered Noah from the great flood. Yet, with the devastated world around him as a reminder of God's grace, he soon fell into drunkenness. After God delivered David out of all his troubles, he fell into adultery and contrived murder. After God delivered Hezekiah from death, he fell into carnal pride and boasting. Even in the midst of God's blessings, no one is safe unless he keeps close to God. He alone is able to keep us."[187]

Safety from Satan is first of all based on making a decision to watch for his attacks throughout the day. *Watch unto prayer*, exhorted Peter.[188] It may be a surprise to detect his work at first. When this excitement wears off, however, that watchfulness is a chore and becomes wearisome. This sense of weariness in watching for Satan's attacks will also be used by him to

187   Owen, *Sin and Temptation*, 80.
188   1 Peter 4:7.

attempt to distract our attention from the truth. He will cause one to feel that it is too difficult to maintain this watchfulness or that one is exaggerating the problem. These lies only serve to weaken our defense. If the truth is maintained as the only foundation for our thoughts and conclusions, we will notice that those Satan-inspired conclusions are false.

It is true that forming a new habit of being constantly aware of the danger of Satan's attacks and of watching for them is not easy or natural. This habit is spiritual in nature and requires strength and power. God himself provides this power through the person of the Holy Spirit, so we know the truth that, although it is difficult to form this new habit, it can and must be done. We know the truth that Jesus would not have commanded us to watch and pray if this were too difficult to achieve. We must believe Jesus and trust in the power of the Holy Spirit. This is our victory: Truth, the Holy Spirit, and faith in both. When we are focused on God's truth and believe it, and when we trust in the power of the Holy Spirit, a sense of resting in him relieves us from the weariness, and we are prepared to not only continue watching but also to do spiritual battle.

Battle

The final step in overcoming Satan's temptation is to do spiritual battle against him. Paul uses words that describe this personal battle. He says we *wrestle*,[189] and we must *withstand*,[190] and he speaks of the *weapons of our warfare*.[191] This does not imply a passive knowledge of Satan but rather an active battle against him. "Not to conquer sin is to be conquered by sin" says Owen.[192] Later he urges, "Rise up with all your strength against the first

---

189 Ephesians 6:12.
190 Ephesians 6:13.
191 2 Corinthians 10:4.
192 Owen, *Sin and Temptation*, 21.

suggestion of sin, and be no less indignant about it than if it had already accomplished its aims."[193]

Jesus demonstrated this active battle during his temptation. He not only rejected the lies and temptation, he used Scripture against Satan to destroy his lies and resist him. He commanded him to retreat, saying *get thee hence.*[194]

We must imitate this tactic of warfare as Stanley says, "The lesson is unmistakably clear. If the only One who ever lived a sinless life combated temptation with God's Word, how do we hope to survive without it? I am so glad He did not outsmart Satan in a battle of the minds. I have tried that and failed miserably. I am glad He did not discuss the temptation with Satan and resist him that way. Eve tried that, and she got nowhere. I am glad Jesus did not use raw willpower, though I imagine He could have. My willpower is pretty useless when Satan really turns on the steam. Jesus verbally confronted Satan with the truth; and eventually Satan gave up and left."[195]

James 4:7 says *Submit yourselves therefore to God. Resist the devil, and he will flee from you.* In C. S. Lovett's excellent book, *Dealing with the Devil,* he describes how this command to resist means to fight.[196] He recommends that we follow the example of Jesus by quoting Scriptures directly to Satan as a weapon against him and by the authority we have through Jesus' name, commanding him to *Get thee hence.*[197]

---

193 Owen, *Sin and Temptation,* 180.
194 Matthew 4:10.
195 Stanley, *Winning the War Within,* 133.
196 Lovett, *Dealing with the Devil,* 86.
197 Lovett, *Dealing with the Devil,* 108.

CHAPTER 12

The Holy Spirit

Jesus' example of facing temptation shows us how truth is our foundation for victory. However, Matthew tells us that Jesus was led by the Holy Spirit.[198] Any experience in overcoming temptation as a normal practice will depend upon the Holy Spirit's work as well as the knowledge of truth. Many sincere Christians who have a broad knowledge of God's truth are still defeated by temptation, often due to the lack of the power of the Holy Spirit in their lives.

Owen points out, "The Holy Spirit is the only sufficient means for the work of mortification [of sin]. All other ways are futile without Him. In vain do men seek other remedies. Vows, fastings, and other efforts of spiritual discipline mean little if the Holy Spirit is not present."[199]

Of course, even this is a matter of truth, so truth covers every need to set us free from temptation's dominance. The point that needs to be made here is that we find in God's Word that it is possible to depend upon one's own power instead of the power of the Holy Spirit, and that one's own power, the power of the flesh, is unable to win victory over temptation.

Paul revealed these two sources of power to the Galatians saying *Are ye so foolish? having begun in the Spirit, are ye now made perfect by the flesh?*[200] This question leads us to consider what source of power we are depending upon and to understand

---

198   Matthew 4:1.
199   Owen, *Sin and Temptation,* 161.
200   Galatians 3:3.

our absolute dependence upon the Spirit. Earlier we discussed the problem of a person not sensing his need of God (page 20).

Jerry and Kirsti Newcombe remind us of this crucial point: "If we believe that we can handle everything all by ourselves and don't need anybody's help, we close ourselves off to God's help. It is through admitting our own insufficiency that we open the communication channel to heaven. And when we cry out to God, He is always available."[201]

This weakness of the flesh occurs during periods of time which we called the comfort zone, when there are few or relatively light trials and problems. Sometimes it occurs after major accomplishments or victories that tend to lead us to overconfidence (page 24). Either way our sense of total weakness is not clear or apparent. There seems to be natural strength, although we do not actually think about the source of our strength. In this state of mind, we are, in reality, without strength, and there will be no power to prevent a fall when temptation comes. We must learn and remember our absolute need of God's power that is given to us through the Holy Spirit.

Knowing our need, however, is not the complete answer. Once our need and dependence upon the power of the Holy Spirit is clear, we must make use of that power through an act of our will.

Owen describes this relation of our own will and the power of the Spirit, saying: "Second, mortification [of sin] must remain a work of our obedience to His Spirit. It is a work that preserves our free will, so we must do so with our understanding, will, affection, and conscience. He works in us and with us—not against us, nor in spite of us, nor without us. His assistance is an encouragement to our desires."[202]

We have learned that the will is the prize God seeks. When

---

201   Newcombe, *A Way of Escape*, 41.
202   Owen, *Sin and Temptation*, 162.

our will is guided by truth and is absolutely dependent upon the Holy Spirit for power, it is capable of deciding and acting in a way that God will honor with the experience of that power. Paul taught the Galatians this principle when he said, *This I say then, Walk in the Spirit, and ye shall not fulfill the lust of the flesh.*[203] Overcoming temptation, therefore, is founded upon the knowledge and acceptance of truth, but is dependent upon walking in the Spirit.

It is significant that Chapter 8 of Paul's epistle to the Romans, which perhaps more than any other passage in the Bible speaks of the Christian's victory, mentions the Holy Spirit nineteen times. From the very beginning of the chapter, Paul relates victory over the flesh to the power of the Spirit, saying: *There is therefore now no condemnation to them which are in Christ Jesus, who walk not after the flesh, but after the Spirit. For the law of the Spirit of life in Christ Jesus hath made me free from the law of sin and death.*[204] Our mind and life must be occupied with the Holy Spirit if we desire to overcome temptation. He will work through our conscience to give light and meaning to God's truth, and he will make that truth our experience through his power.

What then is required of our will to experience the power of the Holy Spirit? Many things can come to mind as a possible answer to this question. Submission would seem to be the obvious answer and is mentioned by James as a requisite to resisting the Devil: *Submit yourselves therefore to God. Resist the devil, and he will flee from you"*[205] Yet the whole problem is that we are tempted not to submit and many times are overcome with this temptation. Submission therefore is not the most basic means to the victory but rather is the victory itself. What is the means to

---

203 Galatians 5:16.
204 Romans 8:1-2.
205 James 4:7.

the victory that our will is capable of fulfilling? Many Christian authors and preachers say the answer is to ask God to fill us with the Holy Spirit according to Luke 11:13, which says, *If ye then, being evil, know how to give good gifts unto your children: how much more shall your heavenly Father give the Holy Spirit to them that ask him?* Yet, in reality, some ask to be filled with the Holy Spirit and experience victory while others ask to be filled with the Holy Spirit and do not experience victory. What makes the difference? James says that asking is important, but that it is not the whole point. He says *ye have not, because ye ask not. Ye ask, and receive not, because ye ask amiss.*[206]

---

206 James 4:2-3.

CHAPTER 13

Faith

As we study these questions and requirements of the will, we find that an act of the will always qualifies our asking and is inherent in true submission. *Faith* is this underlying act of the will. When a person prays in faith to be filled with the power of the Holy Spirit, he will not have the sense that his prayer will mystically result in his filling, but will rather be trusting that God will do whatever it takes to give him the strength he needs. Jesus shows that faith is the qualifier when he says, *And all things, whatsoever ye shall ask in prayer, believing, ye shall receive.*[207] This coincides with John's declaration that, *this is the victory that overcometh the world, even our faith.*[208] Just as faith is the means to salvation by grace through the Lord Jesus Christ, so also faith is the means to victory over temptation through the power of the Holy Spirit.

Owen eloquently declares, "To act in faith on the fullness that is in Christ to supply all our needs is a wonderful way of abiding in Christ. Let your soul declare: 'I am a poor weak thing: unstable as water, I cannot excel spiritually. The corruption of the flesh is too hard for me to cope with by myself. I have been deceived too many times to believe that I have finally obtained victory over sin. I am tempted to say, 'My way is hid from the LORD, and my judgment is passed over from my God.' Yet I know that 'the everlasting God, the LORD, the Creator of the ends of the earth, fainteth not, neither is weary? there is

207   Matthew 21:22.
208   1 John 5:4.

no searching of his understanding. He giveth power to the faint, and to them that have no might he increaseth strength' (Isaiah 40:27-29). He assures us that His grace is sufficient (2 Corinthians 12:9)."[209]

It is impossible to overestimate the importance of our faith to God. Hebrews 11:6 says that *without faith it is impossible to please him.* Romans 14:23 says, *whatsoever is not of faith is sin.* What could be of greater importance in our lives, in our relation to God, and for our hope of well-being?

God has given us the truth through his Word and the power through the Holy Spirit, but our part is to exercise faith through our will. We must remember that these elements are interrelated and inseparable. Faith is our responsibility, yet it comes by *hearing and hearing by the Word of God.*[210] Faith is an act of obedience on our part and a fruit of the Holy Spirit's work in our lives.[211] Our will must obediently exercise faith, and yet faith is what drives our will to obey. We might think of an automobile to see the interdependency of these factors that are required for victory. The engine is the truth. It must be correctly engineered and in good condition. The Holy Spirit is the gasoline that gives power. Faith is the electric current that ignites that power, and our will must turn the switch. This illustration, of course, does not attempt to fully demonstrate the importance and interrelation of truth, the Holy Spirit, faith, and our obedient will.

Faith means believing and trusting. When we believe God's Word, we see it as absolutely superior to any thought or purpose we might have. Even though we are tempted to disobey, there is no doubt in our minds that the outcome of our ways will be as the Word of truth admonishes us. When we have

---

209   Owen, *Sin and Temptation,* 189-190.
210   Romans 10:17.
211   Galatians 5:22.

faith in the Word, our mind is focused on truth, which ruins the conditions that Satan seeks to develop to do his deceitful work. Satan knows this and will attack our faith with doubts and false reasonings.

Screwtape instructed his demon nephew, "Another possibility is that of direct attack on his faith. When you have caused him to assume that the trough [period of dullness or dryness] is permanent, can you not persuade him that 'his religious phase' is just going to die away like all his previous phases? Of course there is no conceivable way of getting by reason from the proposition 'I am losing interest in this' to the proposition 'This is false.' But, as I said before, it is jargon, not reason, you must rely on. The mere word *phase* will very likely do the trick."[212]

Stanley also describes the need for faith and Satan's attack against it, saying: "Satan has many believers convinced that it is a waste of time to try to resist temptation. They believe it is only a matter of time and they will fall. Why go through the frustration of trying if failure is unavoidable? So they surrender without a fight.

"That attitude can develop if you do not accept the fact that *God puts a limit on the intensity of your temptation.* Despite your past experience, you must accept by faith that God will not allow you to be tempted beyond what you are able to bear. Think about it. Since you have been a Christian, every temptation you have faced thus far could have been overcome. The same is true for the temptations you face from now on. No matter how difficult this may be to comprehend, you must accept this premise if you are to build an effective defense against the enemy."[213]

Faith in the Holy Spirit involves trusting not only God's ability, but even more so, his heart. We trust not only that he

---

212 Lewis, *Screwtape Letters*, 51.
213 Stanley, *Winning the War Within*, 78.

can help us because he is powerful, but that he *will* help us because he is good and merciful.

Owen says, "First, we will experience the reality of the grace and compassion of God. He calls the fatherless and the helpless to rest upon Him. No soul has ever lacked God's supply when he depended upon God's invitation to trust in Him absolutely."[214]

This is an important point, as faith will be incomplete and weak without understanding this. We do not have full faith in God if we do not trust in his goodness as well as in his power.

Faith is Action

As mentioned before, faith is an act of our will. It does not just happen, as if it were a simple emotion. Many people excuse their unbelief because they expect faith to mystically appear. Others live in distress that they cannot believe because they also are waiting for faith to just happen. We do not always notice the act of our will in choosing to believe. At times, when we hear the truth, faith results so quickly and naturally that our will does not seem to be involved. Faith is a command of God, however, and any command involves our will, and we have no excuse not to trust in God and his Word. We can choose to trust him.

Just as love is described in the Bible as not being a matter of feeling but rather as a matter of decision and action,[215] faith is described in the same way. Faith is not just felt, it is exercised. The two elements that Jesus commanded in order to avoid temptation, watchfulness and prayer,[216] are acts of faith. We watch and pray because we believe what he said.

We can attempt to watch and pray as an act of our will alone in response to his command. This is not only possible but common and natural. It is the difference between living

---

214 Owen, *Sin and Temptation,* 123.

215 1 Corinthians 13.

216 Matthew 26:41.

according to the law and living according to grace. If our will is exercised to obey as a response to the law, we will not have the power of the Holy Spirit and will fail to overcome temptation. Our will must be exercised as an act of faith in God's truth and in the power of the Holy Spirit in order to experience victory over temptation.

Prayer

Prayer is an act of faith which is both protection against temptation and victory itself. As an act of faith, prayer pleases God and touches his heart, motivating him to respond with his power, protection, and mercy. God himself instructs us in his Word to *come boldly unto the throne of grace, that we may obtain mercy, and find grace to help in time of need.*[217] Jesus taught his disciples that prayer is one of the most important practices that will protect us from temptation. Twice he exhorted them in the garden of Gethsemane, saying: *Pray that ye enter not into temptation* [218] and again later, *Why sleep ye? Rise and pray, lest ye enter into temptation.*[219] Prayer puts us in the safest condition possible. We are in communion with God, and although Satan attacks even during prayer to get our minds on other worldly things, these thoughts are easily distinguished because of our focus on God, and they can be quickly rejected.

On this, Owen advises, "But as I have said before, do not allow your thoughts to dwell upon the things that tempt you (that only causes further entanglement), but set yourself against the temptation itself. Pray that the temptation will depart. When it is taken away, you may more calmly consider the things that tempted you."[220]

Our sense of power is renewed as we see our flesh as weak

---

217 Hebrews 4:16.
218 Luke 22:40.
219 Luke 22:46.
220 Owen, *Sin and Temptation*, 134.

and unworthy of being our guide, while at the same time trusting by faith in his power to guide us and give us victory through the Spirit.

Again, Owen correctly explains, "Second, the effect of this *gives the heart a deep, full sense of the vileness of sin* and a constant renewed sense of detesting it. This is one purpose of prayer—to present sin before us, drawing out its vileness, abomination, and seriousness, so that it is loathed, abhorred, and therefore cast away as a filthy garment (see Isaiah 30:22). He who pleads with God for the remission of sin also pleads with his own heart to detest it (see Hosea 14:2-3). In this way, sin is judged in the name of God. It also confirms to the soul that God detests sin and passes sentence. Prayer, then, sensitizes our soul against sin, so that it will not be bribed or confirmed secretly by sin for even a moment. This leads to the weakening of indwelling sin in the believer."[221]

Self-Discipline

Self-discipline must also be exercised as an act of faith. When exercised according to our own ability, some strength may be apparent due to a strong will, family culture, or a sense of respect for one's reputation. However, we will be just where Satan wants us in spite of the appearance to the contrary. We will do things our way, even as we call it God's way, and will have no promise of victory. When self-discipline is an act of faith, however, our will is resting in God's power and person and not in our own. The discipline we have developed as a result of our parents' discipline is a wonderful experience as long as it is a part of his plan and a tool in his hands. Respect for our reputation is no longer weakened by self-concern but is strengthened by a spiritual concern for God's honor. Even when a person has been raised without correction by his parents and

---

221   Owen, *Sin and Temptation,* 47.

has not developed self-discipline, a true, humble, pure faith is capable of transforming the most disorderly life into one of order and self-discipline, which will build a new reputation.

The Bible contains numerous illustrations of men and women who exercised self-discipline as an act of faith. These must be followed not only as examples of obedience, but as acts of faith. Job is one of the best examples. He had faced the fact that as a man he was susceptible to the temptation of attraction to women. Because of his faith in God's will and ways, he had made a conscious pact with his eyes to use them in a way that would honor God and would not fulfill the desires of the flesh.[222] All Christian men can and should exercise their faith in God's ways by consciously making this pact with their eyes. By faith, we trust the superiority of God's will for our lives and rely upon the power of the Holy Spirit to fulfill this work in our experience. As we continue to keep this pact by faith, we will experience the *way of escape* that God gives to overcome temptation. Job had been so victorious and faithful in this pact that, without fear, he could open himself up for scrutiny in this area and say, *If mine heart have been deceived by a woman, or if I have laid wait at my neighbour's door; Then let my wife grind unto another, and let others bow down upon her.*[223]

In the same way, Job had put his trust in God as his provider and, in spite of his riches, had not changed that act of faith. In this area also he had overcome the temptation to make money his source of security and his sense of success. He could truthfully declare, *If I have made gold my hope, or have said to the fine gold, Thou art my confidence; If I rejoiced because my wealth was great, and because mine hand had gotten much; If I beheld the sun when it shined, or the moon walking in brightness; And my heart hath been secretly enticed, or my mouth hath kissed*

---

222 Job 31:1.
223 Job 31:9-10.

my hand: This also were an iniquity to be punished by the judge: for I should have denied the God that is above.[224]

Isaiah the prophet also taught that practical acts of self-discipline, exercised by faith in God, would result in victory and satisfaction, saying: *He that walketh righteously, and speaketh uprightly; he that despiseth the gain of oppressions, that shaketh his hands from holding of bribes, that stoppeth his ears from hearing of blood, and shutteth his eyes from seeing evil; He shall dwell on high: his place of defense shall be the munitions of rocks: bread shall be given him; his waters shall be sure.*[225]

Paul is a prime example of a New Testament character who practiced self-discipline by faith. He felt the same desires and temptations as any man but demonstrated his practical discipline of the natural appetites when he said, *But I keep under my body, and bring it into subjection: lest that by any means, when I have preached to others, I myself should be a castaway.*[226]

One of the ways he disciplined his body was by fasting often with praying.[227] Fasting is a personal discipline taught by the Lord himself when he was teaching about giving and prayer.[228] He said that fasting would be rewarded by God when it was practiced by faith in his will and not for the glory of men. This practice of abstaining from eating for some period of time was practiced frequently by godly people in both the Old and New Testaments. Even though fasting is mostly associated with earnest and fervent prayer in times of turmoil, affliction, or important events and decisions, it is also an obvious discipline of the body. The person who fasts learns to submit his will to the Spirit and deny the natural appetites of the body. As fasting is practiced, the ability to deny the natural appetites is

---

224   Job 31:24-28.
225   Isaiah 33:15-16.
226   1 Corinthians 9:27.
227   Acts 13:3; 14:23.
228   Matthew 6:16-18.

recognized and becomes a reality. When one develops this ability to deny the body's appetite for food, one can also deny the body's appetites for sensual gratification and other weaknesses of the flesh. This discipline is extremely effective in overcoming temptation and can be one of the most important acts of faith in experiencing victory.

Again, personal discipline that is an act of faith in God's Word and the power of the Holy Spirit is a victory over temptation, but it is also a continual protection to avoid or overcome temptation. Peter exhorts the readers of his epistle to practice this self-discipline and overcome temptation, saying: *Dearly beloved, I beseech you as strangers and pilgrims, abstain from fleshly lusts, which war against the soul.*[229] By faith in the Word and in the Spirit, this experience will become a reality.

Control of Curiosity

We have discussed the relation of natural curiosity to temptation, and we found that curiosity can lead to temptation. This is a principal area requiring self-discipline as an act of faith in God to restrain this natural tendency from becoming a tool of Satan. The danger of exposure to people or circumstances must be understood and definite, practical steps must be taken to avoid such exposure (page 8). We have outlined areas where adjustments can be made to reduce the risk of incorrect curiosity (page 12-17). If a serious desire to overcome temptation and enjoy the freedom of spiritual living exists, these areas should be reviewed and adjustments made as a definite, practical step toward victory.

The innate strength of natural curiosity probably cannot be changed due to its genetic basis. Intelligent awareness, however, always brings greater capacity for self-control. A person who is unaware of his high innate curiosity will not even know

229   1 Peter 2:11.

about his need for self-control and will merely act on a natural instinctive plane. Giving in to his curiosity will be considered natural. However, if he becomes intelligently aware of how the strength of curiosity varies between temperaments and sexes and where he personally fits into the scale, he will be able to see his greater need to exercise self-control. This will result in an adjustment to the scale of curiosity that is exercised, even though the scale that is innate remains unchanged.

The remaining five areas can all be adjusted, because they are based on circumstances and behavior. In considering developed interests, one will have the tendency of placing more attention on developing interests in areas where curiosity can be given its full rein to accomplish positive achievement. Interests in areas where curiosity can result in temptation and sin can and must be minimized or eliminated by substituting the positive areas. Again, this involves intelligent awareness and definite purpose to achieve the goal in practical daily living.

The possibility factor, meaning the difficulty or ease with which an activity or purpose can be accomplished, can be adjusted through planned, purposeful changes. These can be as simple as removing certain objects, games, literature, and so forth from the home, or in canceling subscriptions, or other things that lead to curiosity in areas that lead to temptation. On the other hand, it may involve drastic, life-changing adjustments, as a change in school, work, or even community and church. Being aware of this "possibility factor" allows one to focus clearly on the way one's circumstances are affecting personal behavior and make the necessary changes clear, practical, and achievable.

The next two variables in the formula, the known-unknown and the experience factors can be confused with one another as a matter of semantics. They are interrelated but are not really synonymous. The basic difference is a matter of time and place. The known-unknown factor has to do with the present circumstance, whereas the experience factor has to do with the memory and influence of previous circumstances. The adjustments that are possible to the known-unknown factor can and probably will be based on instruction received from the Bible and other authoritative and trustworthy sources. Abstaining from all *appearance of evil*[230] and being *simple toward evil*[231] are exhortations dealing with this factor. Through the instruction of the Bible, godly men and through the experiences of others, we can reduce the attraction of the unknown. The stories of Samson and David, especially in regard to the consequences of immoral behavior, can enlighten the mind of a young person to create a strong resistance to curiosity about immorality. The end result becomes clear and undesirable, even though there has been no personal experience. I do not need to "open the closed drawer" because someone trustworthy has told me what is inside and the satisfaction of my curiosity will not be desirable in the end. On the other hand, testimonies or instruction about positive and desirable consequences can make me want to "open the drawer" as far as good is concerned. Therefore, adjustments in this variable will have to do with instruction and direction in order to make clear the ways of life and what the final consequences are.

On the other hand, I use the term "experience factor" to refer to previous circumstances in one's own life. This factor may be the outcome of success in the previously considered known-unknown factor. The more good instruction that is trusted and followed, the more positive experience there will be, and the more negative experience will be prevented. However, our formula deals with curiosity about an object or activity in actual life experience on a scale of 1–10. For instance, the person

---

230   1 Thessalonians 5:22.
231   Romans 16:19.

who has never had experience drinking alcoholic beverages will have a much lower level of temptation than someone who has had a previous habit of drinking. The person who does not know about the magazine section at the drugstore will have little curiosity about it, as opposed to the person who has seen them. Adjustments to this factor in the formula involve previous experiences in relation to activities in which one can be tempted to do wrong again. Obviously, previous experiences are history and cannot be changed. What can be changed are the attitudes toward the experiences and future occurrences.

A man in one of my mission churches had lived in many immoral and worldly experiences during his teen years. However, after he was saved as a young adult and experienced a great change for good in his life, he erroneously concluded that worldly and immoral activities as a teen are not a serious problem. He "came out all right," so why be so concerned with his children's worldly desires? As he sat before me agonizing over the stained reputation of one of his children, he realized how erroneous his attitude had been. When he finally saw how many people were scarred for life and destroyed by the sin sown in their youth, he recognized that it was only by God's grace that he had been saved and that he would have lost his life and soul except for that grace. When his attitude toward his experience changed, the direction of his family did as well, and this brought about a change in their future experience.

This altered outlook and attitude toward wrongful habits is crucial in order to achieve new direction and experience. Addiction to alcohol, drugs, or even pornography is usually reinforced by attitudes of inadequacy, anger, despair, and so forth. These often result in a defense of the behavior or a denial of the addiction. Any true hope of a change of experience depends upon a change in attitude about the experience.

Besides the need for a different outlook, there is also the need for new, positive experience. Discontinuing or at least diminishing a wrong practice will leave a vacuum that must be filled with some substitute experience. Otherwise, the tendency will be to go back to known practices. The parable of the reformation of a man as told by Jesus in Matthew 12:43-45 illustrates this principle in relation to salvation. Jay Adams refers to this problem in relation to a Christian's need to experience both the putting off of old ways and the putting on of new ways:

"When God forgives a repentant sinner, He never leaves the matter there. Forgiveness not only marks an end, it is a watershed that also constitutes the beginning of something new. God insists that the matters which the repentance concerned must *be cleared up.* That is to say that true repentance at length will bear "fruit" that is appropriate to it. This fruit always involves change. Change in human relationships not only leads to the abandonment of the old ways (putting off), but also the establishment of a new relationship (putting on). The new relationship may develop out of a request for (or offer of) help following the granting of forgiveness (cf. Ephesians 4:28, 29 and comments in *Competent to Counsel,* pp. 228 ff.). If a new relationship based upon biblical change and help is not established, then it is likely that one or more of the parties will revert to his old ways again. If so, again an unreconciled condition will develop. This failure frequently results in a kiss-and-make-up pattern. The same old problem is never really settled but becomes the reason for continued and repeated confrontation, confession, and forgiveness. The answer to this problem lies in the concern to take steps immediately to establish a new biblical relationship between the offender and the offended party once forgiveness has been granted."[232]

This is based upon the Scripture found in Colossians 3:8-14,

---

232 Jay Adams, *The Christian Counselor's Manual* (Grand Rapids: Baker Book House, 1973), 63-64.

But now ye also put off all these; anger, wrath, malice, blasphemy, filthy communication out of your mouth. Lie not one to another, seeing that ye have put off the old man with his deeds; And have put on the new man, which is renewed in knowledge after the image of him that created him: Where there is neither Greek nor Jew, circumcision nor uncircumcision, Barbarian, Scythian, bond nor free: but Christ is all, and in all. Put on therefore, as the elect of God, holy and beloved, bowels of mercies, kindness, humbleness of mind, meekness, longsuffering; Forbearing one another, and forgiving one another, if any man have a quarrel against any: even as Christ forgave you, so also do ye. And above all these things put on charity, which is the bond of perfectness. Therefore it is clear that active planning of new practices is essential to achieving change in experience, which in turn will adjust this factor in the level of a person's curiosity. I remember Bill Gothard describing this principle in his *Institute of Basic Youth Conflicts* (now, *Basic Life Principles*). He used the term "cycles of life" to show how these wrong experiences relate to other circumstances that come up at certain times of a day, week, or month. Tempting thoughts, circumstances, or imagined possibilities will remain in the mind as "bunkers" of temptation that will assault the mind time after time at certain periods or under certain circumstances. As wrong responses are repeated, tendencies develop and finally habits are formed. The solution given is to purposely plan a different response or experience when that time or circumstance comes up again. Each time change in experience occurs the strength of the habits will diminish, and eventually they will be broken. A continuing new experience will form new patterns or tendencies, resulting finally in new habits.

Jerry and Kirsti Newcombe comment on this tendency of failure leading to more failure, and success leading to more success, saying: "However, I have found that both success and failure in curbing a particular sin leads to further success or failure in that area. Usually, there's either habitual victory or downward spirals."[233]

The last element in the formula is the reward factor. As we have seen, the reward factor relates to a sense of benefit or satisfaction that is associated with the results of an activity. Adjustments to this factor in the formula require a clarification of just what those supposed benefits are. This is not a simple task, because many people do not consciously understand what it is that they find desirable about some activity. Values or rewards are found in many classes. Some are easy to see and understand, such as sensual experiences, monetary gain, power, or popularity. Other rewards are more difficult to explain. These may involve emotions of joy, feelings of self-worth, or relief from the negative emotions of guilt, shame, or inferiority. Even vengeance may be the satisfying reward. Sometimes it requires a good depth of experience and discernment with sincerity and honesty to determine just what a person's values are in order to make adjustments to these values and reduce the strength of curiosity in areas of wrong.

Jesus dealt with this reward factor when he taught us to *lay not up for yourselves treasures upon earth . . . but lay up for yourselves treasures in heaven.*[234] The apostle Paul declares this change in values in Colossians 3:2, saying: *set your affection on things above, not on things on the earth.* The first need then is to discern honestly what one's values are and then learn what is right and wrong with these values. When intelligence and conscience come into play, values can change.

In some cases this is simply a matter of instruction. If someone is ignorant of right and wrong or has been deceived in some way, he may need authoritative and trustworthy instruction to

---

233 Newcombe, *A Way of Escape*, 11-12.
234 Matthew 6:19-20.

become wiser in the area of right and wrong and the resulting values. Sometimes it is not a matter of ignorance, but rather of focus. David was not ignorant of right and wrong when he sent for Bathsheba. He was merely focused on the desired delight and so was blinded to the truth of what was to be valued. When the temporal satisfaction was over, however, reality came back into view with all of its terrible consequences. Adjustment of the reward factor, therefore, also involves an opening of the mind to see the complete picture with all of the supposed benefits and the harmful consequences. This broader scope of understanding with complete moral instruction is what can effect a change in values or, as we have termed it, the reward factor.

By breaking down the force of curiosity into these factors, we can find practical steps of action for ourselves or for others we are helping in order to find change, lessen temptation, and overcome its power in our lives. It is helpful to find and include relevant questions related to these factors and include them in the formula as a practical work page. For example:

Factor	Scale

Innate Strength_____

Have I studied temperaments to discover mine?

What temperaments are strongest in me?

How will this affect my curiosity scale?

How will my sex affect my curiosity scale?

Does this seem apparent to me?

Does this seem apparent to others?

How watchful do I need to be on a scale of 1-10?

What specific areas of wrong provoke my curiosity?

What has God promised that will help me find strength and victory?

Developed Interests_____

What areas of my personal interests can lead me to wrong?

What do I do in my free time?

What do I do when alone?

How does a person become interested in something?

What can I do to discover other positive areas of interest?

Who can help me in this?

Possibilities_____(Remember the drawer.)

Curiosity about which of the above interests is easy to satisfy?

Why is it easy to satisfy?

Are there objects involved in making this more possible?

How can these objects be removed or substituted in order to remove the possibility of provoking this curiosity?

Are there activities or places that make this more possible?

How can these activities or places be changed or avoided?

Are there people that make this more possible?

What changes need to be made in these relations?

Known/Unknown_____(the miniskirt)

What is my attitude about knowing about things that are wrong?

Is this attitude in accord with the Bible?

Are there circumstances in my life that expose me to the desire to know about wrong?

What can I do about these circumstances to avoid such exposure?

Are there people who expose me to this desire?

What can I do about these relationships to avoid such exposure?

Experience_____ (cycles of life)

What experiences have awakened my curiosity toward wrong?

Can the circumstances occur again?

What would be the correct response?

What steps could I take to achieve that correct response?

What circumstances can be simply eliminated?

Do the circumstances have to do with particular people?

What needs to be done about these relationships?

Reward_____

What areas of wrong provoke my curiosity?

What is the attraction or reward of these areas?

How do they fulfill me physically, emotionally, materially, and socially?

Why do I value this type of fulfillment?

What good will this do me in one year, ten years, and eternity?

Do I practice thinking about the consequences or about the harm that may result?

What harm can result in my life or in the lives of others?

What harm is physical, emotional, material, social, spiritual?

What examples do I have in the Bible? In my life? Others' lives?

What are the rewards of positive behavior in all these areas?

What or who influences my values?

TOTAL_____

These questions are simply examples. Each individual can probably think of many other helpful questions. The point is that by minimizing each factor's influence toward wrong and by maximizing each factor's influence toward right, the total curiosity level can be adjusted, which will change the degree of temptation experienced. This leads to a life of less shame and harm.

Loyalty

Loyalty is another quality that results from faith in God's will and ways. God teaches us to honor those authorities that he has placed over us and to serve them honestly. When this service is considered a part of God's plan and, therefore, the right thing to do, a special relationship develops with these authorities that is based on our relationship to God. This sense of desire to do right toward God and toward those people he has placed over us is called loyalty. When we are tested with temptation that involves doing wrong against God or one of these authorities, the demonstration of loyalty is also an act of faith. How this quality of loyalty can also protect us from falling to temptation is illustrated in the life of Joseph. He had served Potiphar faithfully, and a good relationship had developed due to Joseph's faith that doing the right thing in serving was always the correct and best course of life. Potiphar developed a trust in Joseph, and Joseph developed this sense of loyalty. When Potiphar's wife attempted to seduce him, his sense of loyalty to God and to Potiphar restrained him from that temptation, as we find in Genesis 39:8-9: *But he refused, and said unto his master's wife, Behold, my master wotteth not what is with me in the house, and he hath committed all that he hath to my hand; There is none greater in this house than I; neither hath he kept back any thing from me but thee, because thou art his wife: how then can I do this great wickedness, and sin against God?*

God once desired to show Israel how disloyal they were to him. He did this by showing them a demonstration of what loyalty is, using the family of the Rechabites as an example. Jeremiah was sent to bring this family to the temple of God. When they arrived at this obviously special and important meeting, they were given wine and cups by God's prophet and told to drink. In spite of the sense of importance of the occasion and their respect for this man of God, they refused. The reason given was their loyalty to Jonadab their father who, due to the degenerate condition of the people of Israel, had commanded them not to drink wine or build houses or plant vineyards, but rather to live in tents as strangers and not become like the sinful people of their nation.[235] Their loyalty restrained them from associating with evil influences and protected them from temptation, and it became a testimony that God used as a message to the whole nation.

Loyalty is not only shown in relationships to authorities but also in other relationships that are defined by God, such as to a wife and family or a church or nation. When one is loyal in these relationships according to God's plan and will, this sense of loyalty will be a powerful protection against temptation. We must note, however, that this loyalty must be toward God first and according to his will in the other relationships. When there

---

235   Jeremiah 35.

is loyalty to relationships and authorities that are out of God's will, it can become the cause of falling to temptation rather than the cause of overcoming.

Public Identification

Another act of faith that is a powerful force against certain temptations is the matter of public identification with Christ, including his church and his way of life. When a person, by faith, gives testimony of his relationship to the Lord and his church, he feels a great sense of duty to demonstrate his sincerity and a great desire to avoid the appearance of being a hypocrite. This can be a powerful force to resist temptation.

Another act of faith, which is similar to public identification, is that of establishing a relationship or group to whom one will be held accountable for his thoughts and actions. This principle of establishing accountability has already been discussed (page 123) and should be reviewed and considered as a priority if there is a sincere desire to overcome temptation.

Service

Since temptation is so connected to the state of our mind and emotions, we need to develop a lifestyle where these will have positive influences. One way to experience this positive motivation is to form a lifestyle of habitual service for God and man. Serving God and others is not only a sacrifice that benefits his work and their lives; it also brings a tremendous benefit in our own lives. When we experience the joy and satisfaction of serving, our minds become more focused on positive, godly purposes, and our emotions find a source of fulfillment in good, spiritual activities. This reduces the idleness and boredom in life that Satan uses as an occasion to fill our minds with incorrect thoughts or tempt us to seek fulfillment in worldly activities. We are doing ourselves, our families, and our churches a great favor when we plan definite, habitual ways to serve God and others. Marriages will find new unifying purposes. Children will experience activities that will fulfill their needs while also directing their lives toward noble paths. Churches will enjoy a spirit of sharing a common purpose and the fellowship that results. Above all, as these circumstances become a reality, many temptations are avoided and eliminated, and others lose their attraction. Instead we experience the fruit of Paul's exhortation that *if ye then be risen with Christ, seek those things which are above, where Christ sitteth on the right hand of God.*[236]

---

236 Colossians 3:1.

CHAPTER 14

God's Divine Protection

As we act by faith in God's Word and in the power of the Holy Spirit, we can rest by faith in God's divine protection. If we desire to overcome temptation and live in a way that is pleasing to God, how much more must God himself desire this victory for us. In his Word, we do not find that he merely demands our obedience and blesses or disciplines according to our success in overcoming temptation. Rather, we find that he has a tender love for us and desires our well-being much more than we do. Our present state of living in a condition with temptation, weakness of the flesh, the deceit of the world, and the evil work of Satan is part of a plan that has a reason, a cause, and a purpose. This exposure to temptation can be limited, but it cannot be eliminated. However, God understands the struggle, and although his intervention is limited to responding to our acts of faith, we can rest assured that he has a way of intervening for our good solely as an act of his own mercy and goodness.

This tender and profound desire for our protection and the willingness to intervene is seen throughout the Bible. In a time that Israel was falling away from God, he put his protection around her saying to Hosea, *Therefore, behold, I will hedge up thy way with thorns, and make a wall, that she shall not find her paths.*[237] When Jesus prayed for his disciples before his betrayal and crucifixion, this desire of his heart was expressed to the Father, saying: *And now I am no more in the world, but these*

---

237   Hosea 2:6.

are in the world, and I come to thee. Holy Father, keep through thine own name those whom thou hast given me, that they may be one, as we are.[238] We find it comforting and important for our faith to understand that overcoming temptation is not a result of our faith alone, but also of God's own merciful work in our lives. We must not forget our responsibility to believe and act by faith. God's mercy will not be shown as a substitute for our lack of faith. However, we must remember that even in those times when we fail to believe, *yet he abideth faithful: he cannot deny himself.*[239]

Prevention

This divine intervention involves three methods: Prevention of temptation, limitation of temptation, and deliverance from temptation. When it is his will, God can prevent temptation. This is probably more common than we know. Just as Satan can use circumstances to incite our emotions or passions, so God can and does use circumstances to put out the flames of those emotions or passions. When he wants to, he can destroy desires that might lead us to temptation. Of course, even his general plan for our lives includes circumstances that are for our protection. Nothing is more practical for preventing temptation than the instructions given to the Corinthians by Paul when he said:

> *Now concerning the things whereof ye wrote unto me: It is good for a man not to touch a woman. Nevertheless, to avoid fornication, let every man have his own wife, and let every woman have her own husband. Let the husband render unto the wife due benevolence: and likewise also the wife unto the husband. The wife hath not power of her own*

238 John 17:11.
239 2 Timothy 2:13.

body, but the husband: and likewise also the hus-
band hath not power of his own body, but the wife.
Defraud ye not one the other, except it be with con-
sent for a time, that ye may give yourselves to fasting
and prayer; and come together again, that Satan
tempt you not for your incontinency.[240]

His ways for our lives not only give us protection from temptation but victory as well. However, in addition to the protection that is part of his general plan for our lives, he also prevents temptation by direct intervention. He can remove someone from a certain place and put distance between him and tempting circumstances. At times, sickness can accomplish this purpose as in the case of Paul's *thorn in the flesh* that was allowed to prevent the temptation of pride.[241] When Jesus spoke of his disciples being branches of the vine that would be purged by God to *bring forth more fruit,*[242] he revealed God's direct intervention to purify us and strengthen us. One result of this purging is also that we are more protected from temptation.

Owen says, "God uses *providential events* for the same purpose. These may be positive or negative in character. Positively, God causes the soul to desist from sin—and its lustful pursuit—by affliction. He chastens men with bodily sickness, to turn them from their purpose, and to hide sin from them (see Job 33:17-19). God sometimes visits them with adverse circumstances to their reputation, their relationships, their fortunes, and to other desirable things. Finally, He showers and heaps such mercies upon them that they realize once more from Whom these blessings come and yet against Whom they are rebelling.

"Negatively, God may actually hinder some from their pursuit of sin."[243]

240 1 Corinthians 7:1-5.
241 2 Corinthians 12:7.
242 John 15:1-5.
243 Owen, *Sin and Temptation,* 32-33.

Limitation

Prevention is not always part of God's plan, but limitation of temptation is. He promised us that, *There hath no temptation taken you but such as is common to man: but God is faithful, who will not suffer you to be tempted above that ye are able; but will with the temptation also make a way to escape, that ye may be able to bear it.*[244] This passage gives us hope of having a *way of escape* and demonstrates that God is constantly intervening for our good and victory.

Deliverance

Finally, God's intervention includes deliverance when we are experiencing the battle with temptation. Peter wrote, *The Lord knoweth how to deliver the godly out of temptations, and to reserve the unjust unto the day of judgment to be punished.*[245] He was referring to the example of Lot who was unwise in his self-serving decision to choose the fertile plains around Sodom and Gomorrah, take up residence in Sodom, and expose himself and his family to grave temptation. However, God saw the struggle in Lot's heart and the torment that the temptation caused him because of his desire to do well, and God intervened to deliver him from temptation. This example was given to all Christians who feel tormented by temptation and truly desire to overcome.

> Jerry and Kirsti Newcomb cite D. L. Moody's declaration: "The trouble is, people do not know that Christ is a Deliverer. They forget that the Son of God came to keep them from sin as well as to forgive it."[246]

---

244 1 Corinthians 10:13.

245 2 Peter 2:9.

246 Newcombe, *A Way of Escape*, 3.

Conclusion

One of the most well-known passages in the Bible dealing with our struggle to overcome temptation is Paul's exhortation to put on *the whole armour of God.*[247] I end with this key passage because the purpose was to come to this final Scripture and show how the objects of our spiritual armor are manifestations of the three factors for victory over temptation: Truth, the power of the Holy Spirit, and faith. Paul does not use this same list in other epistles because his purpose was not to give a total exposition of all our resources in this spiritual warfare, but rather to give us examples of what it takes to *withstand* the powers and influences of evil. The resources mentioned are: Truth, righteousness, preparation of the gospel, faith, salvation, the Word of God used by the Holy Spirit, prayer, and watchfulness.

Truth in this passage implies both the knowledge of truth and the act of truthfulness. Righteousness, according to Paul's letter to the Philippians, is not our own righteousness according to the law, but the righteousness *which is of God by faith.*[248] In other words, it is that righteousness which has been received by faith in Christ and is experienced by faith in the power of the Holy Spirit. The preparation of the gospel is the act of faith that comes from understanding our purpose in being a witness of God's salvation through faith in Christ. Faith is mentioned alone but is the act of trusting in God's Word and the power of the Holy Spirit. Salvation, as a part of our protection, involves not only the faith that made us sons of God, but also the faith that, being sons of God, we will have the final victory. The Word

---

247 Ephesians 6:12-18.
248 Philippians 3:9.

of God is our foundation of truth that is used by the Holy Spirit to destroy Satan's deceit and free us from his traps. Prayer and watchfulness are also acts of faith.

This passage also establishes the conclusion that if a person desires to overcome temptation, he must learn and understand the many factors involved in Satan's abilities and tactics and his use of the world and the flesh to deceive and seduce. He must learn, understand, and trust the truth of God's Word. He must understand that he can and must act by faith in the power of the Holy Spirit to withstand evil, overcome temptation, and experience the peace, joy, and well-being of living in God's will.

Stanley exhorts, "No doubt you have heard sermons on the armor of God before. This is a very popular passage among preachers. But as familiar as most Christians are with the content of this passage, I find very few who take seriously Paul's application of these verses. Paul did not say, 'Understand the full armor of God.' Neither did he say, 'Research each piece of Roman armor alluded to in these verses.' Paul said, 'PUT IT ON!'"[249]

Finally, one must not become discouraged as he battles against temptation and feels the full power of the enemy. When a person begins this battle against temptation, it is common to feel that he is losing ground instead of gaining. He feels weaker than ever. Understand that this feeling of going backwards is not failure at all. It is simply the experience of more actively facing the power of the enemy.

The Newcombes mention a statement by C. S. Lewis in *Mere Christianity* written during World War II which says: "A silly idea is current that good people do not know what temptation means. This is an obvious lie. Only those who try to resist temptation know how strong it is. After all, you find out the strength of the German army by fighting against it, not by giving in.

---

249 Stanley, *Winning the War Within,* 116.

You find out the strength of a wind by trying to walk against it, not by lying down. A man who gives in to temptation after five minutes simply does not know what it would have been like an hour later. That is why bad people, in one sense, know very little about badness. They have lived a sheltered life by always giving in. We never find out the strength of the evil impulse inside us until we try to fight it: and Christ, because He was the only man who never yielded to temptation, is also the only man who knows to the full what temptation means – the only complete realist."[250]

Do not be discouraged, therefore, by this sense of weakening. You are actually gaining ground in true warfare. Let the truth work to make you free. Keep the faith in God's Word and the power of the Holy Spirit. God means to conquer and you can be a part of that victory.

---

250 Newcombe, *A Way of Escape,* 211-212.

Bibliography

Adams, Jay. *The Christian Counselor's Manual*. Grand Rapids: Baker Book House, 1973.

Lindner, Phil, ed. *Albert Barnes Commentary*. In *Power Bible* CD Version 3.7, Bronson: Online Publishing Inc., 2002.

Bunyan, John. *The Pilgrim's Progress*. 1973 ed. Grand Rapids: Zondervan, 1967.

Lindner, Phil, ed. "Ephod." *Easton's Bible Dictionary*. In *Power Bible* CD Version 3.7. Bronson: Online Publishing Inc., 2002.

The Holy Bible, KJV.

Lewis, C.S. *The Screwtape Letters*. 1941 ed. Uhrichsville: Barbour and Company, n.d.

Lovett, C. S. *Dealing with the Devil*. Baldwin Park: Personal Christianity, 1967.

Newcombe, Jerry and Kirsti. *A Way of Escape: Experiencing God's Victory Over*

Temptation. Nashville: Broadman and Holman, 1999.

Owen, John. *Sin and Temptation: The Challenge of Personal Godliness*. 1996 ed. Minneapolis: Bethany House Publishers, 1983.

Stanley, Charles. *Winning the War Within*. Nashville: Thomas Nelson Publishers, 1977.

Webster, Noah. *First Edition of an American Dictionary of the English Language. 1828*.

Anaheim: Foundation for American Christian Education, 1967.

"Subconscious." *The World Book Encyclopedia*. 1979 ed.

Understanding
& *OVERCOMING*
Temptation

Temptations Traps
& How to Avoid Them

DR. DANIEL MORRIS

An Abstract:

Understanding and Overcoming Temptation

James Daniel Morris

One of the most common struggles experienced by mankind is that of temptation. Both the knowledge and feeling that something is incorrect about a certain activity, whether it is physical, emotional, or intellectual battle against an attraction and drive to go against one's better judgment and do what is wrong. This struggle robs one of peace. If he resists temptation, it fills his mind and emotions with turmoil. If he falls to temptation, it leaves him with the agony of guilt and shame.

Repeated resistance will result in greater strength and peace, whereas repeatedly falling can harden the heart with either despair or a seared conscience. This book attempts an in-depth analysis of the processes involved in temptation and overcoming temptation. It is written with the hope that the reader can gain understanding that will lead him to practical steps toward continual victory over temptation in his life.

The method of research used involves both personal experience from forty-eight years of observing the struggle in my own life and from twenty-eight years of ministry, in which temptation is always a major factor in the challenge to build the lives of others. Aside from personal experience, I examined the Library of Congress to find material from other authors who had, through their personal experience and ministries, written on the subject of temptation. Both my own observations and those gleaned from my sources were written down, organized, and reorganized until the final book took form. Other sources were naturally needed, sought, and included in the course of developing the book, including encyclopedias, dictionaries, and commentaries to clarify and expand on subjects and terminology used.

It was established that understanding and overcoming temptation involves three areas of struggle or "enemies" and three sources of victory. The struggle is with one's own weakness (the flesh), attraction to corruption in the environment (the world), and direct or indirect attacks of a formidable enemy (the Devil). Victory involves a clear understanding of truth and reality which is founded upon the Word of God, the supernatural power needed to compensate for natural weakness which is found in the work of the Holy Spirit, and that which connects us to that truth and power of the Holy Spirit, which is our faith in both.

Major findings include the significance of natural curiosity in the process of temptation. Natural curiosity, which is so useful for creative problem-solving and progress in humanity, is also a principal factor in temptation to do wrong. Understanding this problem leads one to many practical disciplines to cultivate positive results of curiosity and stifle the negative results that can cause damage.

Other major findings include the significance of the mind in the struggle with temptation and the importance of the conscience. The mind is the center point, or battleground, in temptation. Since truth is discerned in the mind and Satan strives to influence the mind any victory over temptation must include a depth of discernment of these processes. In particular, one must understand the critical importance of the conscience that is the sensor that God placed in man to detect and differentiate between right and wrong. When functioning correctly, the conscience is a crucial part of victory. However, this sensor is delicate and can be mishandled or damaged to the point where it may not function correctly or function at all.

When the full scene is understood regarding the extent of the weakness of the flesh, the attraction and deceit of the world, and the subtle, calculated attacks of Satan, a bleak picture appears that seems to be an insurmountable problem. God has allowed this seemingly insuperable condition to demonstrate how much more potent is his Word and power, which can be accessed by mankind if they believe and act according to that faith. He has promised in no uncertain terms that there is a *way of escape* in any temptation, and mankind can discover and experience that victory.

About the Author

D r. Morris was raised in a church planting ministry in California and has now served in the ministry himself for nearly forty years. For the last 36 years, he has worked as a missionary in the southernmost region of Mexico. His primary missionary work has involved starting new churches and leading them to start more churches. He has also been involved extensively with training pastors, teaching seminars, counseling individuals and families, and developing an in-depth, three-year discipleship program for pastors and church members. He received his Bachelor of Arts degree from Pacific Coast Baptist Bible College (now Heartland Baptist Bible College) under the direction of Dr. Jack Baskin, his Masters from Anchor Theological Seminary and his Doctorate from Louisiana Baptist University. He and his wife, Debbie, have raised four children who serve the Lord, and they live in Tuxtla Gutierrez, Chiapas in Mexico.

Also by the Author

Ethical

What You Must Know to Build Trust
and Maintain Genuine Relationships

DR. DANIEL MORRIS

The Christian desire to honor God and be faithful to him is the most important reason for learning and practicing what is ethical. We should understand that nothing could be wiser, more appropriate, and more secure than God's way of thinking. For this reason, living an ethical lifestyle will not be done out of an attitude of sacrifice, but out of a feeling of appreciation and desire for God's will.

Ethical addresses topics such as:

- Knowing When to Obey or Counter Authority
- Ethical Care of Things Owned by Others
- Ethical Handling of Finances
- Making and Adhering to Ethical Promises
- Proper Behavior With the Opposite Sex

Why You Really

can

Memorize
Scripture

Understand
and unlock your
mind's natural
ability to memorize
long passages.

DR. DANIEL MORRIS

Understand and unlock your mind's natural ability to memorize long passages

Called to be a missionary as a teenager, I had a great desire to fulfill God's will, but had a great sense of inadequacy for such an extraordinary purpose. But God says he who meditates in His Word ... *shall be like a tree planted by the rivers of water, that bringeth forth his fruit in his season; his leaf also shall not wither; and whatsoever he doeth shall prosper* (Psalm 1:3). This verse was and still is a great source of encouragement.

Part of meditation is to memorize God's Word, so I began a systematic method of memorizing consecutive passages of scripture. Through the years I learned, both by study and by experience, how God made our memory function. Presently, I have 42 chapters memorized and, best of all, our missionary work has prospered beyond what I could have imagined.

This book describes what I learned about permanently memorizing scripture and will help you be one of the few who experiences the blessing of meditation in God's Word, and the hope that *whatsoever he doeth shall prosper.*

In this book you'll learn:

- Specific memorization techniques.
- How to memorize scripture, the Bible.
- How to retain what you memorize

CPSIA information can be obtained
at www.ICGtesting.com
Printed in the USA
LVHW01s1959270917
550255LV00001B/8/P

9 781622 452361